Julia Vorl

Towards a Culture

Interethnische Beziehungen und Kulturwandel

Ethnologische Beiträge zu soziokultureller Dynamik

herausgegeben von

Prof. Dr. Jürgen Jensen, Universität Hamburg

Band 65

LIT

Julia Vorhölter

Towards a Culture of Participation?

The Influence of Organizational Culture
on Participation and Empowerment
of 'Beneficiaries'

A Case Study
of a Social Organization in Pretoria

LIT

To the girls of Lerato House

My special thanks to the Tshwane Leadership Foundation and the German
Academic Exchange Service (DAAD) for supporting my research.

Bibliographic information published by the Deutsche Nationalbibliothek
The Deutsche Nationalbibliothek lists this publication in the Deutsche
Nationalbibliografie; detailed bibliographic data are available in the Internet at
http://dnb.d-nb.de.

ISBN 978-3-8258-1934-7

A catalogue record for this book is available from the British Library

© LIT VERLAG Dr. W. Hopf Berlin 2009
Fresnostr. 2 D-48159 Münster
Tel. +49 (0) 2 51-620 32 22 Fax +49 (0) 2 51-922 60 99
e-Mail: lit@lit-verlag.de http://www.lit-verlag.de

Distribution:
In Germany: LIT Verlag Fresnostr. 2, D-48159 Münster
Tel. +49 (0) 2 51-620 32 22, Fax +49 (0) 2 51-922 60 99, e-Mail: vertrieb@lit-verlag.de

In Austria: Medienlogistik Pichler-ÖBZ GmbH & Co KG
IZ-NÖ, Süd, Straße 1, Objekt 34, A-2355 Wiener Neudorf
Tel. +43 (0) 22 36-63 53 52 90, Fax +43 (0) 22 36-63 53 52 43, e-Mail: mlo@medien-logistik.at

In Switzerland: B + M Buch- und Medienvertriebs AG
Hochstr. 357, CH-8200 Schaffhausen
Tel. +41 (0) 52-643 54 85, Fax +41 (0) 52-643 54 35, e-Mail: order@buch-medien.ch

Distributed in the UK by: Global Book Marketing, 99B Wallis Rd, London, E9 5LN
Phone: +44 (0) 20 8533 5800 – Fax: +44 (0) 1600 775 663
http://www.centralbooks.co.uk/html

Distributed in North America by:

Transaction Publishers
New Brunswick (U.S.A.) and London (U.K.)

Transaction Publishers
Rutgers University
35 Berrue Circle
Piscataway, NJ 08854

Phone: +1 (732) 445 - 2280
Fax: + 1 (732) 445 - 3138
for orders (U. S. only):
toll free (888) 999 - 6778
e-mail: orders@transactionpub.com

i

TABLE OF CONTENTS

LIST OF ACRONYMS

BA	Beneficiary Assessment
CBNRM	Community Based Natural Resource Management
CDD	Community Driven Development
CTMM	City of Tshwane Metropolitan Municipality
FBO	Faith-Based Organization
GTZ	Gesellschaft für Technische Zusammenarbeit
II	Informal Interview
ILO	International Labour Organisation
INT	Interview
LH	Lerato House
NGO	Non-Governmental Organization
O	Observations
PCM	Pretoria Community Ministries
PH	Potter's House
PID	Personal Identification Number
PLA	Participatory Learning Analysis
PRA	Participatory Rural/ Relaxed/ Rapid Appraisal
PRSP	Poverty Reduction Strategy Paper
RDP	Reconstruction and Development Programme
RRA	Rapid Rural Appraisal
SA	Social Assessment
SARAR	Self-esteem, Associative strengths, Resourcefulness, Action planning and Responsibility
TLF	Tshwane Leadership Foundation
UNISA	University of South Africa
ZOPP	Zielorientierte Projektplanung (Objectives-Oriented Project Planning)

LIST OF TABLES AND GRAPHICS

Tables

Graphics

1. Introduction

"Development defies definition (...) because of the difficulty of making the intent to develop consistent with immanent development. Intentional development (...) consists of the means to compensate for the destructive propensities of immanent change. The difficulty arises because, while an immanent process of development encompasses the dimension of destruction, it is difficult to imagine why and how the intent to destroy should be made in the name of development." (Cowen/ Shenton, 1996: 438)

(Social) development is full of paradoxes. Its benefits and downsides have been and still are controversially discussed in different social science disciplines, though perhaps nowhere as fierce as in anthropology. Although I generally share the skepticism brought forward against development practices, I also believe in and support the overall idea of development (and included in it the idea of development cooperation), namely that in a globalized world those who are "rich and wealthy" (whatever that may entail), cannot be ignorant of the problems and constraints faced by those who are not (Sen, 2000: xi). The means, principles and practices by which international development institutions have tried to realize this idea for the past 50 years have been exhaustively criticized and debated; the ambivalences and contradictions of development have been repeatedly pointed out, especially by post-development critiques. And ever still, there are new ideas, concepts and paradigms evolving in the search of proof for the long envisaged benefits of development and development cooperation.

Currently, participation and empowerment constitute the dominant paradigms in the field of development. Bilateral and multilateral development agencies, NGOs and grassroots movements, all claim to include their "beneficiaries"[1] in the planning, implementation and evaluation of projects, policies and processes. Moreover, they declare that they empower their target groups so that the beneficiaries can eventually help themselves. But despite a general recognition of the importance of participation and empowerment, current mainstream development practices still largely seem patronizing, top-down and blue-print-oriented.

Throughout the course of my academic studies I have followed the debates on development, participation and empowerment. I have gained practical insights into different forms of development cooperation. I have been frustrated but at the same fascinated by the complexities of (participatory) development. And it is this fascination which in the end inspired to me to choose a topic from the field of development as a subject for my M.A. thesis.

---

[1] I use the term "beneficiaries" throughout this thesis to refer to those people who are the target groups of development initiatives. I am aware that "[i]t is no longer common for either NGOs or government donors to speak in terms of 'beneficiaries' or 'counterparts' (...) [as] [s]uch terms imply unacceptable passivity" (Crewe/ Harrison, 2001: 70). Nevertheless, I believe the term "beneficiary" to be more appropriate and comprehensive when talking about the current state of development affairs than more "politically correct" terms such as "clients" or "consumers". For a general insight to the controversies which have been fought within the development discourse about how to define certain terms (and which I will not recapitulate within this thesis) see e.g. Sachs, 1992; Woost, 1997; Arnold, 1996: 82; Cowen/ Shenton, 1996: 438ff.

One thing I have repeatedly noticed throughout my engagement with development cooperation, which became especially evident during my practical experiences, relates to how the structures and cultures of different development institutions influence the outcome of their respective interventions. I became interested in how the various types of organizations – ranging from technocratic to people-centered, from international to local, from professional to idealistic – attempt to implement participatory and empowering development and how their success or failure in doing so is affected by their organizational cultures.

A sweeping example of the relevance of research on organizational culture in modern institutions has been provided by the anthropologist Cris Shore (2005), who analyzed the effects of organizational culture on corruption and nepotism in the European Commission. Moreover, the link between organizational culture and the functioning of an organization currently constitutes a major field of research in business studies. This is due to the fact that companies have realized the importance of culture for their work-efficiency and effectiveness. Managers have come to regard culture as an instrument to motivate staff, to optimize relations between employees, or to convey a certain image of their organization or company to outsiders. In the field of development, the influence of an organization's culture on the outcomes of its work and its functioning has generally been examined less frequently and less systematically. To my knowledge, it has not been systematically analyzed at all with regard to participation and empowerment. This is what I have attempted to do in my M.A. thesis.

As a point of origin, I scanned the vast body of development literature and perused several theoretical and empirical studies on participatory development, critical post-development essays and reflections on alternative development as well as research on NGOs, institutions and social movements. I found that much of the criticism voiced against the current form of participatory development points at or somehow relates to the cultures and structures of the organizations which try to implement it. This insight led me to develop the following two questions which guided my research and which I will try to answer in this work:

1. How does the organizational culture of a development organization influence the way it implements participation and empowerment?
2. What general inferences emerge from the systematic analysis of question 1 for the study and practical application of participatory development?

In my analysis, I have decided on a twofold approach: based on the (anthropological) literature on development and organizational culture, I have developed a theoretical model on how one could link the two variables – organizational culture and participatory development. Secondly, I have applied a case-study approach, based on three months of fieldwork in which I studied a social organization – the Tshwane Leadership Foundation - in Pretoria which is involved in development work. Both, theory and case study, provide evidence for my main conclusions. With regard to the first question I found that four central factors, all related to organizational culture, influence the way an organization deals with participation and empowerment: the organization's degree of professionalization, the values and mission-statement it adheres to, the role of the staff and the organization's ability to learn.

Based on this insight and relating to the second question, I have uncovered what I believe to be two major contradictions which are inherent in the current form of participatory development: to put it in a nutshell, these contradictions are both related to the fact, that only those organizations who are professional and institutionalized have the influence to advance their agendas on a larger scale and to gain access to resources – funds and skilled personnel – which they need to successfully implement their programs. However, the more professional an organization is, the less are the chances that it adheres to the true principles of participatory development. In my final conclusion, this leads me to a rather pessimistic outlook on the realization of the (theoretically) large potentials of participatory development on a broad scale. The study seems to prove once again that "development is built on certain premises that no amount of reform will displace" (Nustad, 1999: 482).

My M.A. thesis is situated within two fields of research in anthropology: organizational anthropology[2] and the anthropology concerned with development. I will briefly comment on both in the following paragraphs.

Organizational anthropology has a long history which goes back to the 1920s. In its early years, the discipline (then called industrial anthropology or anthropology of work) mainly focused on the analysis of industries and businesses. Yet, the exigency for anthropologists to study modern (service) organizations is by no means new. In the early 1970s, Nader (1974) called upon anthropologists to "study up", meaning to study the institutions and organizations which affect people's everyday lives, and not only the people affected by them. Today, the study of institutions and organizations constitutes a major field of research – not only in anthropology but also in many other social sciences. A large body of literature from this research field focuses on the institutions and organizations involved in development work. Anthropologists have only recently taken up this subject. Increasingly however, there are calls for anthropologists to engage in the study of social and development organizations, due to the discipline's special research methods and theoretical approaches (Eyben, 2000; Nustad, 2001: 485ff.; Mohan, 2007: 164; Henkel/ Stirrat, 2007: 183; Bebbington, 2004: 280; Cornwell, 2002: 48f.; Nolan, 1994: 393f.; Russel/ Edgar, 1998: 8ff.; Mosse/ Lewis, 2006; Hutson/ Liddiard, 1993: 34f./ 42f.).

The field of anthropology concerned with the study of development is generally taken to be split into two sub-disciplines[3]. **Development anthropology** is mainly concerned with improving methods and approaches to develop-

---

[2] Throughout this thesis, I make no distinctions between the (related) sub-disciplines "organizational anthropology", "business anthropology" and "anthropology of work". Instead, I use "organizational anthropology" as a collective term.

[3] The boundaries between the two sub-disciplines are blurred rather than absolute and many anthropologists do not position themselves clearly as belonging exclusively to one of the two categories.

4

ment, often by being directly engaged in applied research or in evaluations of projects. Adherents of this sub-discipline generally infer that development cooperation as such is desirable, although probably not in its current form. **Anthropology of development**, on the other hand, primarily engages in "the socioscientific analysis of development as a cultural, economic and political process" (Grillo, 1997: 2) and is generally associated with post-development and poststructuralist approaches. (Friedman, 2006; Nustad, 2001; Grillo, 1997: 1f.; Prochnow, 1996: 21-29). Proponents of this approach often reject all forms of development cooperation (Prochnow, 1996: 28; Mosse/ Lewis, 2006: 2f.).

The "split" of the discipline is mirrored in the anthropological debates on participatory development. Anthropologists are divided on whether participation constitutes just another "tyrannical" (Cooke/ Kothari, 2007) instrument of development, or whether it bears the potential for a more tolerable (and successful) form of development cooperation. In the anthropological literature one can generally discern two types of contributions to the discourse on participation and empowerment: the first type comprises studies on participatory planning methods like PRA[4] as well as discussions of the principles and chances of participatory and empowering development. The authors of these texts aim to contribute to the improvement of participatory development and believe in its potential although they acknowledge and criticize that this has hitherto not been fully realized. The second type of contributions stems from development skeptics who focus (only) on the problems of and criticisms against participatory and empowering development.

This work is not clearly positioned within one of the sub-disciplines of developmental anthropology. On the one hand, it supports the arguments brought forward by development anthropologists – namely that participatory development bears great potentials to improve the current state of development cooperation – and it aims to contribute to the reflections on how the potential of participatory development can be better realized. On the other hand, this work takes a very critical stance on participatory development. Despite the inherent potentials of the approach, it seems that participation and empowerment cannot be applied successfully to mainstream development cooperation due to the structural constraints underlying the latter.

After having outlined the motivation, the main subject and the context of my research, I will now give an overview of the structure of my M.A. thesis.

In the second chapter, I elucidate my research methodology and comment briefly on the methods which can be used and the difficulties which can occur in the anthropological study of organizations.

The third chapter fulfils two purposes: first, it presents a literature review and summarizes current scientific discussions in the field of organizational anthropology (section 3.1) as well as the (more interdisciplinary) discourse on par-

---

[4] PRA stands for Participatory Rural/ Relaxed or Rapid Appraisal; for a detailed description of this popular method see for example Chambers (1994, 1997); Krummacher (2004) and Schönhuth (1996).

ticipatory development (section 3.2). Secondly, I have attempted to link the two research fields and established four concepts which can potentially explain why organizational culture has an influence on the approach organizations adopt to implement participation and empowerment (section 3.3). Nine working hypotheses serve to clarify and accentuate the link between the two variables.

The fourth chapter comprises the case study of the Tshwane Leadership Foundation (TLF) and intends to replicate the structure of chapter 3. I introduce the organization and the field it operates in (section 4.1), before I turn to analyze TLF's organizational culture in more detail (section 4.2). In section 4.3, I depict the operational approach of TLF with special focus on participation and empowerment. Finally, I apply the four concepts introduced in section 3.3 to the case of TLF and assess whether the hypotheses prove to be compelling. The main function of the hypotheses is to render my argument more structured and to draw attention to certain aspects of the complex relationship between organizational culture and participation.

The fifth and final chapter serves to summarize my arguments with regard to the two questions raised above in addition to indicating the achievements and benefits of this study.

2. Research Design and Methodology

2.1 Research Design

The research I conducted is qualitative in nature. Hypotheses on the influence of organizational culture on participation are established (based on a thorough literature review) and their validity is empirically tested in a single unit case study. According to the often cited definition of Yin (1994: 13), "[a] case study is an empirical inquiry that investigates a contemporary phenomenon within its real-life context, especially when the boundaries between phenomenon and context are not clearly evident." Describing the advantages of case studies, Gerring (2004: 350) argues that

"the very 'subjectivity' of case study research allows for the generation of a great number of hypotheses, insights that might not be apparent to the cross-unit researcher who works with a thinner set of empirical data across a large number of units and with a more determinate (fixed) definition of cases, variables and outcomes".

The (comparative) weakness of a case study lies in its "shortfall in representativeness" which renders it less suitable to confirm or disconfirm a theory (ibid: 348ff.)[5]. Thus, my strategy of research is explorative rather than confirmatory. My research approach has descriptive as well as hypothesis/ theory-oriented elements which are often combined in anthropological field studies (Beer, 2003: 17f.). In my empirical part I first *describe* TLF, its organizational culture and its operational approach, before I then employ the four concepts I developed in the *theory* part and test if my *hypotheses* can be successfully applied to the case.

2.2 Techniques and Instruments for Data Gathering

At the beginning of my research, I thoroughly reviewed the literature on organizational culture and on participatory development. The review contributed to the formulation of my research question which then presented the basis for identifying a suitable empirical "case". My decision to select TLF depended mainly on three factors: from what I could infer from the organization's homepage it seemed that TLF adhered to an approach which centered on the principles of participatory development. Secondly, it appeared that the organization was very conscious and candid about its organizational culture and that it would therefore be very feasible to analyze it. Thirdly, TLF was extremely open towards my research and invited me to work as a volunteer in one of its programs as a "participant observer" which would give me full insight into its operations.

Before my departure to South Africa, I carried out a brief and relatively unstructured interview with a respondent who had worked for TLF as a volunteer and through whom I had heard about the organization in the first place. I used this interview to get a first impression of TLF and to explore and discuss how I could apply my research question to the organization. Between July and September 2007, I conducted fieldwork in South Africa. For my empirical research, I chose participant observation and semi-structured interviewing as prin-

---

[5] On the (contested) function of empirical cases and examples ("applications") in a theory and for the confirmation/ disconfirmation of a theory see Lang (1994: 153ff.).

ciples methods. In the anthropological study of organizations, these are the methods most often applied as they are best suited to get a deeper (holistic) understanding of how an organization functions and what role its individual members play (see e.g. the studies of Novak 1994; Götz, 1997; Nauta, 2006; and the volumes edited by Gellner/ Hirsch, 2001; Helmers, 1993; Jones et al., 1988; Russel/ Edgar, 1998)[6]. Furthermore, I collected and analyzed various official and unofficial TLF documents. I met with Skip Krige, who had also carried out research (mainly in the form of interviews) on TLF for his mini-dissertation in development studies. He presented me with some of his research findings and we also discussed my research question. After my fieldwork, I again conducted a literature review and matched my data with what I found in theoretical texts and case studies.

2.2.1 Participant Observation

Prolonged participant observation substantiates "the methodological distinctiveness of anthropological fieldwork" (Hauser-Schäublin, 2003: 33)[7] and is the "heart" of methods for organizational analysis (Wischmann, 1999: 62). It provides different advantages: the researcher does not have to rely solely on the information given to him in interviews, but can prove whether what his informants say correlates with what they actually do. Furthermore, by being inside the organization (for example as a staff member, volunteer etc.), the researcher can gain the trust of his informants and thus get access to information that would not be communicated to "outsiders". Participant observation also reduces the problem of reactivity because as time passes the people who are being "observed" get used to the researcher (Bernard, 2002: 333)[8]. During my fieldwork, I took the role of an "observing participant" (Bernard, 2002: 328) as I was an officially employed volunteer in the organization. *All* of the people I interacted with regularly and most of the other TLF staff knew about my "double-role" as researcher and volunteer. During my working day, I jotted down what I was observing, and at the end of each day I wrote a detailed observation protocol on the computer. I often gained the most interesting insights from spontaneous conversations or "informal interviews" (Bernard, 2002: 204). These presented an important complement to my formal interviews as the informants spoke more openly about current problems and challenges. Through informal interviewing I had the chance to follow up on certain topics which were raised in the formal interviews, or which came up in the day-to-day work. I could also discuss various issues concerning TLF with a great range of people (colleagues, other volunteers,

---

[6] Further important research methods in the study of organizations include situational analysis and network analysis (Wischmann, 1999: 62f.; Diel-Khalil/ Götz, 1999: 92ff.; Russel/ Edgar, 1998: 7f.).
[7] German original: "Die *Teilnehmende Beobachtung* (...) ist die methodische Besonderheit ethnologischer Feldarbeit" (Hauser-Schäublin, 2003: 33).
[8] In this regard, the study of Krige (2007) on TLF exposes some weaknesses. Krige based his analysis mainly on interviews and only attended a few selected meetings and events.

beneficiaries, TLF "outsiders"...) all of whom I could not have interviewed "formally".

In accordance with Novak (1994: 65f.), I consider informal interviews as an important part of participant observation and, therefore, included the information I obtained from these conversations in my observation protocols. In the empirical part of this work, I have marked those analyses derived from direct observations with an "O" (plus date), and those drawn from informal interviews with "II" (plus date). In some cases it was difficult to differentiate between what was concluded from observation and what from informal interviews so I labeled these cases with "O/ II" (plus date). The indication of my observation and informal interview sources (which is often neglected in anthropological studies) constitutes an attempt to render analysis based on participant observation more substantiated.

2.2.2 Semi-structured Interviews

Semi-structured interviews constitute an important supplement to participant observation. They follow a general script and cover a list of topics and therefore provide the researcher with an excellent means to explore certain topics in more detail (Bernard, 2002: 2005; Spradley, 1979). Throughout my fieldwork I conducted ten semi-structured interviews, one of them being a group interview[9], with two basic groups of informants: first, TLF staff, and secondly, TLF beneficiaries. In the selection of my interviewees I (mostly) used "purposive sampling" (Bernard 2002: 182ff.). With regard to the first group, job position constituted the most important criteria for selection. I wanted to speak to the manager of PCM[10] as well as to the coordinators of the four constituent programs or "ministries" of PCM. I also considered it relevant to speak to the (German) manager of the volunteer program (who is also responsible for communications and public relations) mainly because of her knowledge of the difficulties which can occur in the context of "intercultural development cooperation" and her year long experience with TLF – first as a volunteer and then as a fulltime employee.

The interviewees of the second group were beneficiaries from two of the TLF projects[11]: Lerato House (a shelter for girls) and Potter's House (a shelter for women). I chose beneficiaries from these two projects as they had the closest and most frequent interactions with the TLF staff. Concerning the Lerato House beneficiaries, the choice of my informants depended on the length of their stay at Lerato House (excluding those girls who had only been there a few weeks), their age (all three informants were at least 16), their openness towards me and their willingness to be interviewed. In the selection of the Potter's House benefi-

---

[9] The interview was carried out with three beneficiaries from one of the TLF projects (Potter's House), and was based on a semi-structured interview schedule. The interview was very instructive because interesting group discussions evolved and revealed different (and similar) opinions of the beneficiaries on certain issues.

[10] PCM constitutes the "pillar" for social development projects within TLF. For reasons which are explained in section 4.1.2 I chose PCM as the prime unit of my analysis.

[11] On overview of the different TLF projects will be presented in section 4.1.2.

ciaries I relied on the help of a Potter's House staff member who chose three interviewees she thought suitable for me as I did not know most of the women staying there very well ("snowball sampling"; Bernard, 2002: 185f.).

I recorded and transcribed all the interviews (including the unstructured interview I conducted before my fieldwork). In the empirical part I use "INT" (plus identification code) to refer to information obtained from the interviews.

2.3 Data Analysis

All in all, my analysis is based on two different forms of (qualitative) data: first, my empirical data consisting of 60 observation protocols (one for each day of participant observation), ten (transcribed) semi-structured interviews, one (transcribed) unstructured interview and various TLF documents. The second set of data which I will refer to as "theoretical data" originates from the literature review.

In the analysis of my empirical data, I at first adhered to a grounded theory approach (Bernard, 2002: 462ff.). I already started analyzing some of my data during my fieldwork in order to make out recurring themes and identify contradictions or aspects I had not completely grasped. This enabled me to focus my observations and complement my interview guide with important questions I had not previously considered. After my return, I started to analyze my data systematically. This entailed reading through and coding all the interview transcriptions and observation protocols in order to identify central themes and potential analytic categories ("inductive coding"; Bernard, 2002: 464f.).

After this first round of coding, I revisited my theoretical data and engaged in another, more systematic literature review which centered on the themes I had identified in my empirical data. Based on the literature I built my theoretical model and formulated key hypotheses on the influence of organizational culture on participation and empowerment. I also developed a preliminary outline for my M.A. thesis.

Then I went back to my empirical data and coded it a second time, using the rubrics of my preliminary outline as codes ("deductive coding"; Bernard, 2002: 464). The passages extracted provided the foundation for the empirical part of my work in which I used several exemplary quotes to illuminate my theory (on the important function of exemplar quotes see Bernard, 2002: 471ff.).

2.4 Limitations of the Study

Data reliability, deference effects and ethical considerations constitute common problems of research (Bernard, 2002: 141). With regard to my empirical research, the relatively short time of fieldwork (measured by anthropological standards), the fairly low number of interviews and the focus on one section of the organization – PCM – are all factors which limit the explanatory power of the study. Many of my findings were, however, confirmed by the research of Krige (2007), thus strengthening the reliability of my data. During my research, I could sometimes identify deference effects, which evolve when informants give false or inaccurate information (Bernard, 2002: 230ff.). However, participant observation compensated for some of the inaccuracies caused by deference. I often had the chance to observe (or confirm with other people) whether what the informants had said was true.

In anthropology, several debates about the ethical responsibilities of a researcher have been fought, and are still fought today[12]. In the field of organizational research, several anthropologists have expounded common ethical conflicts which a researcher may have to confront when studying "inside" an organization (O'Neill, 2001; Murdoch, 2003: 508f.; Novak, 1994: 22ff. Schein, 2004: 211ff.; Wischmann, 1999: 34f.). During my fieldwork, I often found myself in role conflicts which were related to being researcher and employee, friend and observer, insider and outsider at the same time. I tried to deal with these role conflicts by always being honest and transparent about my research to the people I interacted with. In my analysis, I did not explicitly refer to situations and happenings which were reported to me in confidential conversations. I abstracted my analysis to avoid exposing potentially detrimental information and made the identities of my informants anonymous.

---

[12] For a concise summary see Antweiler (2002).

11

3. Participation and Organizational Culture: Literature Review and Theoretical Foundations

The following chapter builds on an extensive literature review. In the first part (section 3.1), I will give a brief overview of organizational culture research, focusing mainly on anthropological approaches. The second part (section 3.2) summarizes the discourse(s) on participation and empowerment. In the third and most important part (section 3.3), I develop four concepts which suggest that organizational culture influences how an organization deals with participation and empowerment.

3.1 Organizational Culture
3.1.1 Contemporary Research on Organizations
Recently, the study of organizations (and business enterprises) has developed into an important research field within social science. One can identify different reasons for this: on a very general scale, large inter-governmental organizations and transnational businesses have developed into major players in world politics and economics; some even claim that they now exercise more power than single nation states. The same applies to NGOs – they are becoming more and more influential both on the national and international level (West, 2003: 5ff.; Ebrahim, 2003: 1) – and this explains why there is a growing field and, according to Frantz (2005: 21), a sub-discipline of NGO research. The greatest amount of research on NGOs is found in the field of development studies (ibid: 31).

More specifically, the concept of organizational culture has gained prominence, especially in the field of anthropology and business studies[13]. In anthropology this has to do with the expansion of the discipline to incorporate also the study of people in western[14] societies ("anthropology at home"). As people in industrialized societies spend more and more time at work – that is in organizations and businesses – it is of increasing relevance for anthropologists to analyze their workplaces and –cultures (Helmers, 1993: 7; Wischmann, 1999: 4; Franzpötter, 1997: 12f.; Hodson, 2004: 6/ 12). In the field of business, theorists and managers have come to acknowledge that success in business depends not only on rational economic strategies, but also on "soft factors" such as culture and the relationships between staff. A number of popular science books also take up this subject with great success[15] (Wischmann, 1999: 47f.; Senge, 1990: 11; Novak, 1994: 14f.).

Many researchers ascribe great relevance in the study of organizations to anthropology – due to the discipline's special methodology and research prem-

---

[13] For a very extensive review of the literature on organizational culture see Martin et al. (2004).
[14] Throughout this thesis, I use the terms "West" or "western" to refer to those "part[s] of the world contrasted historically and culturally with the East or Orient; the Occident" (The Times English Dictionary, 2000: 1732).
[15] Among the most often cited are the publications of Peters/ Waterman (1982) and Deal/ Kennedy (1982). The popularity of their appealing ideas about the relevance of culture for the management of organizations led Martin et al. (2004: 7) to conclude that the "renaissance of interest in culture began with [these] publications".

ises. They especially value the holistic and interpretative approach, the potential of "thick description" as well as the field methods such as prolonged participant observation and qualitative, semi-structured interviewing. Anthropological approaches are celebrated for being critical, inductive and for focusing (more) on conflicts, dynamics and power relations rather than on a static depiction of the organization. The majority of research conducted in the anthropological study of organizations is to date qualitative, although there are also popular quantitative methods such as network analysis[16] (Diel-Khalil/ Götz, 1999: 85ff.; Wright[1], 1994: 3ff.; Jordan/ Dalal, 2006; Hamada, 1994: 4ff.; Hirsch/ Gellner, 2001: 6ff.; Nauta, 2006: 150f.; Wischmann, 1999: 5ff.; Russel/ Edgar, 1998: 3; Mosse, 2001).

The following section will provide a brief overview of the history of organizational research in anthropology and will then outline concepts and definitions which have been influential in the (anthropological) study of organizations. Lastly, a working definition of organizational culture will be presented which will serve as the foundation on which the relationship between organizational culture and participation will be assessed in the following chapters.

3.1.2 A Short History of Organizational Anthropology

The beginning of anthropological research in organizations and organizational culture can be traced back to the 1920s.

The so-called **Hawthorne Studies**, conducted by psychologist Elton Mayo in an electricity plant between 1924 and 1933, portray the beginning of sub-discipline of organizational anthropology which was then known as industrial anthropology. Mayo and the anthropologist William Lloyd Warner, who was a student of Radcliffe-Brown, applied anthropological methods when they thoroughly observed and interviewed workers on a shop floor (which they treated as a small society) in order to understand the functions of informal organization and its effect on worker productivity. Throughout their study they discovered the importance of socio-psychological factors and human relations on working processes and outcomes. The Hawthorne Studies also presented the beginning of the human relations school in anthropology. In 1930 Warner and Low conducted the **Yankee City Studies** in a shoe factory and demonstrated the hitherto ignored interrelations between work, society, family, organization, social status and community by analyzing a situation of conflict (a worker's strike). In its early years organizational anthropology focused on the study of industries. In 1936, Warner and Gardner established the **Committee of Human Relations in Industry** and in 1946, the two anthropologists set up a consulting company called Social Research Incorporated. The often cited **Manchester Shop Floor Studies** carried out by Max Gluckman and his students in five different workplaces in Manchester aimed at analyzing the influence of informal group structure on work outputs. For the first time the researchers used "real"

---

[16] Severe "methodological battles" have been and still are fought between proponents of quantitative and proponents of qualitative research in the field of organizational studies. These „battles" have been ingeniously recapitulated by Martin et al. (2004: 24ff.).

participant observation (they were employed in the places they studied) in the analysis of workplaces. Their findings highlight the influence of the external cultural environment of the work place and demonstrate that organizations cannot be understood by merely analyzing their formal, internal structures (Wischmann, 1999: 19ff.; Wright[1], 1994: 5ff.; Hamada, 1994: 10ff.; Novak, 1994: 25ff.).

Wright[1] (1994: 14ff.) dates the separation of anthropological and business organizational studies to the 1960s whereby the former shifted towards a more interpretative analysis and the latter remained concerned with a positivist and rational research approach to organizations. Only in the 1980s and 1990s were the two fields recombined through the "culture concept"[17] (Smircich, 1983; Martin et al.: 6f.). Despite this fairly long history of organizational anthropology, in Germany the sub-discipline is only slowly finding its way into mainstream anthropology. This may, to some extent, be due to a general skepticism in Germany towards the field of applied anthropology (Schönhuth, 2002: 1ff.)[18]. The beginnings of organizational anthropology in Germany can only be dated to the 1990s and are associated with the publications of Helmers (1993), Novak (1994) and Götz (1997).

3.1.3 Concepts and Definitions of Organizational Culture

Organizational theorists have borrowed the concepts and definitions of culture from anthropology[19]. The multiplicity of competing definitions of culture in anthropology has reflected on efforts in organizational theory to define "organizational culture" and therefore explains to some extent the sometimes contradictory meanings implied in the term (Wischmann, 1999: 8ff.; Schein, 2004: 11ff.). These have provoked extended debates in the field of organizational research (Hamada, 1994: 4; Wright[1], 1994: 17ff.; Martin et al., 2004). The most fundamental point of discussion which is summarized in numerous publications (e.g. Smircich, 1983; Wright[1], 1994: 17ff.; Novak, 1994: 13ff.; Wischmann, 1999: 11ff.; Hamada, 1994: 21f.; Franzpöttter, 1997: 17ff.) concerns a differentiation between a functionalist understanding of culture (organizations *have* culture) and an anthropological/ sociological understanding of culture (organizations *are* cultures). The former in which culture is depicted as a clearly identifiable and predictable element in organizations, shared by all members, is prevalent mainly

---

[17] The culture concept was first introduced by Smircich in 1983 in one of the most often cited essays in the organizational culture research field and marks a shift in the root metaphor ascribed to organizations. Whereas these were formerly portrayed as machines or as organisms, organizations then came to be regarded as a form of human expression and thus as cultures.

[18] One indicator of this skepticism is that also that one often searches in vain for a chapter on applied anthropology in German introductory volumes to the discipline, for example in the often cited Introduction to Anthropology (2006), edited by Fischer and Beer or in the introduction by Bargatzky (1997).

[19] The anthropological definitions of culture most often cited in organizational studies stem from functionalism (e.g. Malinowski) and structural functionalism (e.g. Radcliffe-Brown) and more recently from cognitive anthropology (e.g. Goodenough) and symbolic anthropology (e.g. Geertz) (Wischmann, 1999: 13ff.; Smircich, 1983: 347ff.).

14

in economics and business studies. According to this understanding, culture is a tool (for the management) which can be used to render the organization more efficient. The latter, labeled the "cultural metaphor" by Smircich (1983), implies a manifestation of culture not only in visible (material) aspects and ideologies but also in more fundamental norms and values which transcend the narrow organizational context. Culture is seen as a social phenomenon, consisting of continuous negotiations, conflicts and ambiguities, which cannot be controlled or managed.

However, as Smircich points out, one does not have to agree on a single definition or concept of culture as these always depend on the research question (see also Martin et al., 2004: 31f.).

"[D]ifferent conceptions [of culture] give rise to different research questions and interests. The differences in approach to the organization-culture relationship are derived from differences in the basic assumptions that researchers make about both 'organization' and 'culture'. Thus, the task of evaluating the power and limitations of the concept of culture must be conducted within this assumptive context" (Smircich, 1983: 339).

3.1.4 Working Definition of Organizational Culture

In the following, a working definition of how organizational culture shall be understood in this work will be developed, relying on different concepts, mainly from anthropology.

According to Hamada (1994: 26f.) organizations are "socio-cultural entities" which develop and persist in a specific historical context and have to be analyzed with regard to their external influences. In one way, organizations *are* cultures – they resemble ethnic groups and can therefore be analyzed with traditional ethnographic field methods[20]. But one always has to bear in mind a central difference between an organization and an ethnic group: whereas members of the latter constitute a "reproduction unit", membership in an organization is defined by staff selection and recruitment procedures and is therefore deliberate, temporarily bound and can be revoked.

Organizational culture consists of various segments. These have to be identified and accommodated in a holistic and complex analysis of culture as demanded by ethnographic principles (Diel-Khalil/ Götz, 1999: 85ff.; Novak, 1994: 24). In the literature one finds several attempts to discern those segments of organizational culture in order to render the concept operative for an empirical analysis (Schein, 2004: 25ff.; Wright[1], 1994: 17f.; Wischmann, 1999: 11ff.). The definition of organizational culture applied in this work draws on the typology of Novak (1994: 23) who differentiates between material culture (e.g. buildings, artifacts, dress etc.), social culture (e.g. hierarchies, rules, communication,

---

[20] Some anthropologists explicitly transfer analytical categories (e.g. language, census etc.) and theoretical concepts (e.g. conflict, power, patronage etc.) used in research on ethnic groups to describe and analyze what is happening in organizations (Wischmann, 1999: 58ff.; Novak, 1994: 61f.; Diel-Khalil/ Götz, 1999: 115).

15

work processes) and spiritual[21] culture (e.g. values, norms, beliefs), whereby all three are interrelated and the boundaries between them blurred.

With regard to the above-mentioned debate about the degree to which organizational culture can be enforced (by the management), I support a twofold approach. I believe that some parts of organizational culture can be intentionally established and managed. These include, for instance, official hierarchies, regular rituals (e.g. meetings) and dress codes. But there are also a number of uncontrollable and often unwanted influences on an organization's culture: deviating behavior of members from the official norms and rules, the development of subcultures as well as conflicts between groups or individuals within the organization, to name a few examples. Despite many non-enforceable and unpredictable elements of organizational culture, I wish to stress that organizational cultures do not develop randomly. Certain, deliberately created features have relatively predictable effects; it makes a difference, for example, whether the management decides to have flat hierarchies or rather installs a rigid, top-down decision-making structure.

Organizational cultures are dynamic and change over time due to internal and external influences (Hamada, 1994: 26f.). This involves constant processes of contestation and consensus-finding, of conflict and consolidation. However, it is usually possible to detect static elements of an organization's culture which persist over long periods of time. Hereby, the institutional environment plays an important role: it structures the way in which the organization is viewed by different societal actors (the government, other organizations, funders, beneficiaries etc.) and thus "forces" the organization to remain somewhat stable in order to maintain its status in the institutional system (Lister, 2003: 178ff.).

The members of an organization are the most important "carriers and formers"[22] of the culture (Novak, 1994: 24; Wischmann, 1999: 10), shaping it through their actions and beliefs. Members who occupy higher positions are usually the most influential, but at the same time the behavior and the actions of all members are to some extent determined by and dependent on the established culture(s) within the organization (Diel-Khalil, 1999: 87). One must also bear in mind that members of an organization, for example staff, are increasingly selected not only because of their qualification, but also to fit into the existing organizational culture so that usually the behavior of new staff does not deviate too far from that of the established members – this is especially the case in faith-based organizations (Frantz, 2005: 177ff./ 196ff.; Beyer and Trice, 1988: 144ff.).

In sum, organizational culture shall in the following be understood as:

---

[21] 'Spiritual' corresponds to the German term "geistig". When applied in the context of organizational culture, 'spiritual' throughout this thesis does not have a religious meaning but refers to the mental or symbolic elements of an organization's culture such as values, rites, symbols, myths etc. which can be best encapsulated by the term 'spiritual'.

[22] German original „Träger und Gestalter von Kultur" (Novak, 1994: 24).

16

1. consisting of a clearly identifiable but constantly changing group of members, defined by the organizational structure as depicted in an organization chart. The culture may be further divided into subgroups – officially (e.g. into departments) and unofficially (e.g. alliances that are founded on friendships, political sentiments etc.). Depending on their status within the organization, individual members have more or less power to influence decisions within the organization and to control other members.
2. having material, social and spiritual components of which some can be managed, whereas others are more uncontrollable and ambiguous.
3. being shaped by the organization's members (dynamic facet), but at the same time influencing the members (and the criteria of their selection) so that some elements of the culture remain stable over long periods of time (static facet).
4. being influenced by external factors such as time, space and the institutional environment.

3.1.5 Concluding Remarks

This chapter has outlined the foundations of the (anthropological) research on organizational culture. These are of relevance to contextualize the case study of TLF (chapter 4) which was influenced by and contributes to this research field. Furthermore, a working definition has been developed which is crucial to comprehend the links that will be explicated between organizational culture and participation in the remainder of this work.

3.2 The Participation (and Empowerment) Discourse[23]

Within the last two decades, numerous theoretical and methodological research papers and case studies have been published on the subject of participation and empowerment in the context of development. The following chapter will try to review the most important aspects of this debate. First, I will present what theorists and development practitioners mean when they speak of participation and empowerment and how these terms are to be understood in this work. Afterwards, the evolution of the participation discourse will be outlined, mainly focusing on how the critical reflections on the many shortcomings of conventional participation approaches have led to the development of new concepts and strategies. Deduced from the review of the participation discourse, four possible interrelations between organizational culture and participation will be suggested at the end of the chapter whose explanatory potential will then be further explored in the next chapter.

---

[23] Citing the prominent definition by Hayer (1993: 45f.), discourse in this thesis shall be understood as an „(...) ensemble of ideas, concepts, and categories through which meaning is given to phenomena. Discourses frame certain problems; that is to say, they distinguish some aspects of a situation rather than others. (...) As such, discourse provides the tools with which problems are constructed." Although I generally speak of *the* (dominant) participation discourse, I imply that there are several "sub-discourses" and "parallel-discourses" which, however, will not be further analyzed in this thesis.

17

3.2.1 Definitions of Participation and Empowerment

As Finsterbusch/ Wicklin (1989: 573) state "the call for participation comes from a broad spectrum of those concerned with development and for a wide variety of reasons." As a consequence there are also varying definitions of what is understood by terms such as participation and empowerment, depending on the reasons why development actors incorporate these elements into their work (Henkel/ Stirrat, 2007: 172f.). The following paragraph gives a brief overview of contending definitions and approaches currently influential in development theory and practice.

The term participation is generally perceived to have a positive connotation, often with a strong normative implication (Beckmann, 1997: 5). Some social scientists identify different levels of participation, depending on how much influence is granted to beneficiaries and to what extent they are involved in decision-making-processes and at what level (Pretty, 1995: 1252; Cornwall, 2003: 1327; Beckmann, 1997: 7). Others differentiate between participation as a means to achieve better development outcomes and between participation as a development objective in itself (Krummacher, 2004: 5f.; Cleaver, 1999: 598; Chinsinga, 2003: 132f.). The former implies a technical understanding of participation. The latter sees participation as a process in which the target group gains new knowledge and awareness which in the end "empowers" the people to influence decisions and policies affecting them (Kievelitz, 1996).

Participation in this work shall be understood as both a method and an aim of development initiatives. The people affected by these initiatives are entitled and enabled to make their own or at least influence decisions in all matters of concern to them. With regard to development projects, participation entails the involvement and consultation of the target groups in all stages of planning, implementation and evaluation. Implicit in this definition is an understanding of participatory development as a long-term, highly complex and in many ways conflicting process in which often opposing ideas and worldviews need to be reconciled[24].

Empowerment is another prominent term in recent development discourses which is only very imprecisely defined. I concur with Krummacher (2004: 6), who summarizes the idea of empowerment as "supporting marginalized and excluded people in handling their own affairs, who by doing so realize their own potential which then enables them to develop own ideas and strategies to shape and/ or improve their living situation"[25].

The concept of empowerment can be traced back to the Brazilian pedagogue Paulo Freire who tried to mobilize politically "the oppressed" by making them aware of their rights. He proposed a radical concept of empowerment

---

[24] The "Arbeitsgemeinschaft Entwicklungsethnologie" (AGEE) suggests a similar definition of participation in their Ethical Guidelines for Development Cooperation (2002: 183).

[25] German original: „(...) benachteiligte Menschen darin zu bestärken, ihre Angelegenheiten selbst in die Hand zu nehmen, sich dabei ihrer eigenen Fähigkeiten bewusst zu werden und eigene Ideen, Strategien und Vorstellungen zur Gestaltung und Verbesserung ihrer Lebenssituation zu entwickeln" (Krummacher, 2004: 6).

which at the time was congruent with alternative development approaches and opposed to mainstream development practice (Freire, 1971 [1970]). Today, social scientists such as Cleaver (1999: 599/ 2007: 37) and Hailey (2007: 99) criticize modern empowerment approaches for having lost the radical, political and alternative nature of former empowerment concepts. This is due to the fact that they have been incorporated into mainstream development thinking.

The blurred concept of empowerment currently discussed and practiced in development cooperation is questioned and criticized on several grounds (see section 3.2.4). The first main point of critique is that it is unclear who should be empowered by whom and how, as the causal relations between (external) intervention, participation and empowerment are rarely reflected upon in the concepts for empowerment projects (Cleaver, 1999: 599; Henkel/ Stirrat, 2007: 170f.). Secondly, it is debatable whether a powerful, external group of actors (such as development practitioners) can empower a group of usually marginalized and "voiceless" people without imposing their own ideas of empowerment on them in a top-down fashion (Mohan, 2007: 164ff.; Henkel/ Stirrat, 2007: 178ff.; Kilby, 2006: 955).

According to some authors, participation leads to empowerment and empowerment in turn leads to new opportunities for participation. In many publications one finds that the two concepts are simply used interchangeably so that both are subject to the same criticisms and praises (Cornwell, 2002: 32f; Henkel/ Stirrat, 2007: 170f.; Cleaver, 1999: 598f.; Hickey/ Mohan, 2004: 168ff.; Chinsinga, 2003: 133; Bliss/ Neumann, 2006: 424). Thus, it cannot be clearly derived from the literature where to draw the line between empowerment and participation approaches, or as Woost (1997: 229) states "... in many ways the discourses of 'participation' and 'empowerment' are not all that dissimilar". In the following, I will mainly speak of participation and the participation discourse, taking the concept of empowerment to be implied.

3.2.2 The Evolution of the Discourse

Ever since the Alternative Development approach in the 1970s[26], participation of beneficiaries has been considered an important component in successfully implementing development projects (Cornwell, 2002: 69f.). In the 1990s "Participation" rose to unprecedented popularity within development cooperation, and up until today it was considered to be one of the dominant paradigms (Chambers, 1997/ 1994)[27]. Some even draw an analogy between participation and religion and claim that participation has become "development orthodoxy" (Cornwell, 2003: 1325), "an act of faith" (Cleaver, 2007: 36) or "spiritual duty"

---

[26] For an insight into the doctrine of alternative development see Krige (2007: 14ff.), Thorbecke (2006: 10ff.) and Freire (1971).

[27] The sudden popularity of participation related to the general acknowledgement that the big (modernization and dependency) development theories had failed (Menzel, 1992). In a time of great frustration and uncertainty among development practitioners and theorists, the participation paradigm gave rise to new optimism within the field of development cooperation (Hickey/ Mohan[1], 2004: 9).

19

(Henkel/ Stirrat, 2007). Some authors express a very critical view on this development as they claim that the ideas that were once "revolutionary (…), anti-colonial and anti-modernization [have] been absorbed into the mainstream of development" (Mansuri/ Rao, 2004: 6; see also Woost, 1997).

Despite continuous criticism of the approaches and strategies to implement participation, very well summarized in the influential volume "Participation: The New Tyranny", edited by Cooke/ Kothari, first published in 2001, nowadays one would rarely find a project proposal which does not explicitly commit itself to participatory development (Cooke/ Kothari, 2007: 3). Although many voices, especially those critical of development cooperation, claim that participation is largely "rhetorical"(Botes/ van Rensburg, 2000: 41; see also Chinsinga, 2003: 129; Midgley, 1986: 3/ 35) and "cosmetic" (Taylor, 2007: 137), a general shift towards a better inclusion of beneficiaries and a more thorough reflection on how these can contribute to a successful project implementation can be noted in current development practices.

As the discourse on participation evolves and new approaches are being explored, the frustration with conventional participation approaches is slowly succeeded by a "new optimism" – instead of being labeled as "Tyranny", participation is associated with "Transformation" (Hickey/ Mohan[1], 2004: title). As with other development paradigms (see Thorbecke, 2006) the evolution of the discourse from the 1970s[28] onwards proceeds cyclically rather than linearly with ideas disappearing and after some years reoccurring again (Cornwell, 2002: 69ff.). However, in the last few years there have been some truly genuine changes in the way participation theorists and (to a lesser extent) development practitioners reflect on the subject (Hickey/ Mohan[2], 2004: 3).

The main focus in earlier debates was on how the effectiveness of development projects in reducing poverty can be enhanced when beneficiaries are included in the planning, implementation and maintenance (Finsterbusch/ Wicklin, 1989: 575ff.). In contrast, proponents of newer participatory approaches recognize the need for "the poor" to participate in decision-making on a broader level due to the structural constraints (political, economic and social) which have to be tackled for poverty reduction to be sustainable. This cannot be achieved by narrowly focusing on projects and programs. A more promising approach would imply moving towards institutional reforms on the local and national level, in which the civil society should actively participate. Therefore, people need to know their citizen rights and have to be given opportunities to express their voices in decision-making-processes. Participation is no longer something granted voluntarily by development agencies to their beneficiaries; it is perceived as a basic human and citizen right (Holland et al., 2004: 225; Gaventa, 2004: 32, Cornwall, 2002: 66ff.; Newling, 2003).

---

[28] Even before the 1970s there have been attempts to include participation as a relevant factor in development work, however these efforts are irrelevant to the research question discussed here and shall therefore not be mentioned further. For an overview of the evolution of the participation discourse since the 1950s see for example Beckmann (1997: 43-64); Krummacher (2004: 8ff.); Mansuri/ Rao (2004: 5-8); Midgley, 1986:13ff).

The new participation discourse recognizes conflicting interests and asymmetric power relations between the different stakeholders involved in development. Therefore, participatory development is no longer seen as a smooth and quick procedure, but rather as a long-term process due to the often opposing ideas which need to be reconciled (Mosse/ Lewis, 2006: 5ff.). Conflict is an immanent part of this process, in which transformation and structural change are seen as two of the most important long-term objectives (Mansuri/ Rao, 2004: 27f.; Cornwall, 2002: 66f.). Institutions play a key role in achieving these objectives as they structure interactions between many different actors and facilitate cooperative behavior (Agrawal/ Gibson, 2003: 6637f.; Cleaver, 1999/ 2007).

In order to put the new theories into practice, participation on project-level (which these days is still the prime focus of development agencies) must be complemented with political strategies. This poses three interrelated challenges to development agencies in order to achieve the institutional and individual changes both necessary for a general transformation of society (Waddington/ Mohan, 2004: 222; Gaventa, 2004: 33): first, empowerment and awareness-raising on human and citizen rights; secondly, support for civil organizations and social movements; and thirdly, strengthening of local and national institutions as well as the government. An effort to react to these challenges can already be identified to some extent in current development approaches (see section 3.2.3).

In sum, one can notice a shift in the focus of the participation discourse from project-centered participation to a broader "citizenship participation". Instead of concentrating on the technical aspects of how to implement participatory development[29] the emphasis is placed more on the political implications of participation. And the target group of development efforts has been rephrased from (passive) beneficiaries to (proactive) citizens and consumers (Cornwell, 2002: 31ff./ 73ff.). Overlapping discourses on democracy, human rights, participation and development are becoming an increasingly interdisciplinary field of research in which the multidimensional nature of poverty, development and democracy as well as the complexity of political and participatory processes is recognized (Holland et al., 2004: 252). However, many of the new insights are to date not or only unsatisfactorily reflected in development practices as will be shown in the following sections.

3.2.3 Approaches to Participatory Development
This paragraph will briefly summarize the most important and influential of development approaches to realize participation and empowerment (a more detailed discussion can be found elsewhere, see references in Table 1). The following constitutes an attempt to categorize the multiple approaches and tools cur-

---

[29] Throughout the 1990s efforts to conceptualize and implement participatory development were centered around participatory instruments with a heavy focus on PRA. This resulted in several publications on the merits and weaknesses of PRA which will not be explicitly discussed in this thesis (Bliss, 1996; Chambers 1997; Richards, 1995; Schönhuth, 1996; Schönhuth et al., 1998).

rently applied by development agencies, which is inspired by Korten's model of strategic action in development (1990: 113-132). Four different (although interrelated) strategies can be identified (see Table 1.), whereby the evolution from participatory research and planning to structural change somehow reflects the learning process within the field of participatory development as described above.

Participatory research and planning techniques are designed and used for identifying the needs and interests of the target group in the planning and initial implementation stage of a project. As mentioned above, the idea behind this is to increase the efficiency of development projects, as experience has proven that top-down and externally planned projects are more likely to fail (Ebrahim, 2003: 38; Taylor, 2007: 127ff.; Platteau/ Gaspart, 1999: 1687). The level of participation in this approach is fairly low as the development agency still "owns" the development process.

Community Development Strategies partly supersede the very narrow project-context as they aim for the participatory implementation and long-term maintenance of sector specific programs (e.g. resource management). They focus on the strengthening of old or (more often) on the building of new institutions at the local level as these facilitate cooperative behavior and present a way to manage interactions in the long run. The development agency acts as a facilitator (this mostly implies providing money and training) and initializes a process which as the program evolves is slowly taken over by the community. Therefore, community development projects are expected to be more sustainable, as the beneficiaries learn to deal with future problems themselves, and are also considered more cost-effective as the people are required to contribute to the projects, mostly in form of labor (Blaikie, 2006: 1944ff; Mansuri/ Rao, 2003).

Institutional Development and collective Empowerment targets the broader community and social structures and is not specifically tied to one sector. Instead, these initiatives aim to make citizens aware of their rights and mobilize them to become socially and politically active. Efforts to support and build civil society initiatives are supposed to result in a growing establishment and spread of a democratic political culture (Van Rooy, 1998; Carothers, 1999; Carothers/ Ottaway, 2000).

Structural change refers to political strategies at the macro-level in which the main actors are large international development agencies (such as the World Bank) and national governments. Introducing new policies is expected to result in social and political transformation. Decentralization, for example, aims at transferring decision-making power to the local level, thus creating better opportunities for local actors to shape development processes (Bierschenk/ de Sardan, 2003: 145).

Strategy	Participatory research and planning techniques	Community Development	Institutional Development and collective Empowerment	Structural change
Methods/ Approaches	RRA, PRA, PLA, ZOPP, BA, SA, SARAR[30]	CDD, CBNRM[31]	Supporting/ building of civil society; rights-based/ advocacy projects[32]	Decentralization, PRSP; influencing policies on the national level[33]
Aim	Identify needs and interests of the target group	Sustainable and long-term maintenance of programs in one specific sector	Initiating a civil society movement	Transformation
Level	Project	Program	Broader community and social structures	Government Level, broader society
Role of Development agency	Implementer	Facilitator	Mobilizer	Political consultant

Table 1: Development Approaches to Participation and Empowerment

3.2.4 Reasons for the Failure of Participatory Development

There are many voices which criticize the underlying ideas of participatory development. Social scientists, as well as development practitioners, have identified several reasons why it fails in so many contexts. With my M.A. thesis I have attempted to contribute to this debate. In addition to conventional explanations, which have been thoroughly discussed in the literature, I argue that one reason for the frequent failure lies in the structures and cultures of development organizations. In order to contextualize my study, it is important to briefly recapitulate the most prominent arguments put up against participation and/ or the way it is put into practice.

The **"myth of community"**: One of the oldest and most frequent points of critique concerns the ideas about "the beneficiary community" found in many project conceptions. The community is pictured as a homogenous, static and spatially bound unit. This narrow and superficial perception ignores internal power asymmetries within the communities, especially along the lines of gender, age and class/ caste as well as conflicting interests between community mem-

---

[30] Chambers (1997), Francis (2007), Schönhuth (1996/ 1998), Kievelitz (1996), Bliss (1996), Beckmann (1997), Krummacher (2004), Richards (1995), World Bank (1996)
[31] Mansuri/ Rao (2003/2004), Platteau/ Gaspart (2003), Agrawal/ Gibson (1999), Blaikie (2006)
[32] Carothers (1999), Carothers/ Ottaway (2000), Waddington/ Mohan (2004), Hickey/ Mohan²³ (2004), Gaventa (2004)
[33] Gaventa (2004), Bierschenk/ de Sardan (2003) Verron et al. (2006), Holland et al. (2004), Hickey/ Mohan²³ (2004), Eberlei (2003), Sehring (2002)

bers[34]. Furthermore, it simplifies or completely overlooks complex analytical concepts such as culture and social capital (Blaikie, 2006; Agrawal/ Gibson, 1999; Hickey/ Mohan², 2004: 11f.; Cleaver, 1999: 603ff.; Mansuri/ Rao, 2003: 8ff.; Botes/ van Rensburg, 2000: 47ff.).

Representation: Who serves as a legitimate representative of a "community" or target group? This is one of the most important, but at the same time most complex problems developing agencies have to solve. Elite capture presents a common obstacle to participatory development as in many cases only the local elites have the time, legitimacy and skills to participate. Discussion sessions, for example, in which development agencies want to identify a community's needs, usually work according to western communication rules. Moreover, they are held in public which prevents community members, especially women, from voicing their opinion as they are not used to and/ or not allowed to speak publicly and usually have other, more subtle mechanisms of influencing community-decisions (Cornwell, 2003: 1328ff.; Agrawal/ Gibson, 1999: 638ff.; Platteau/ Gaspart, 2003: 1688ff.; AGEE, 2002: 184ff.; Botes/ van Rensburg, 2000: 45ff.; Mansuri/ Rao, 2004: 19ff.; Bliss/ Neumann, 2006: 425).

Cooperation with "traditional" local institutions or with newly-founded institutions can both cause unwanted constraints on participatory development. Whereas the former are often a manifestation of local power structures (and inequalities), the latter are usually designed to mirror western institutions – with formal rules and sanctions and a functioning bureaucracy – and are thus not rooted in the local historical, social and institutional context (Cleaver, 2007/ 1999: 600ff.; Richards et al., 2004: 23-26; Richards et al., 2005: 14ff.).

Working with local NGOs at first sights appears to solve some of the above mentioned difficulties. However not all local organizations are serious, professional and accountable. The organizations considered support-worthy by western development agencies usually have an office in the bigger cities, are comprised of highly-qualified, western-oriented staff and are part of the local elite, thus not being much closer to the poor and marginalized target groups than their international counterparts (Woost, 1997: 241ff.; Platteau/ Gaspart, 2003: 1688ff.; Isaacs, 2000; Carothers, 1999; Bliss/Neumann, 2006: 425; Chinsinga, 2003: 137f.; Murdoch, 2003).

"Superficial" Participation: Concepts like participation and empowerment are intrinsically political and therefore cannot be incorporated into development work by merely applying new methods and technologies. Social scientists strongly criticize that the mainstreaming of participatory development has led to a deradicalization and depoliticalization of the approach. They claim that participatory rhetoric is used by development agencies to conceal what in fact still is a top-down development fashion (Waddington/ Mohan, 2004: 220; Cleaver, 1999: 599; Cornwall, 2003: 1327; Woost, 1997: 230; Mansuri/ Rao,

---

[34] For a very good exemplification of the problems which can arise when the intra-communal diversity with regard to age, gender and class is ignored see Richards, Bah and Vincent (2004) and Richards, Archibald, Bevelee et al. (2005) who have analyzed CDD in a post-conflict-setting in Sierra Leone and Liberia respectively.

2004: 6). Some point out the "hegemonic" (Taylor, 2007: 138f.) and "subjective" (Henkel/ Stirrat, 2007: 178) nature of participation by which the powerful try to conceal the prevailing power structures (see also Nustad, 2001).

The problem of structural change: Development experts have come to realize that their prime aim – abolishing poverty – can only be achieved by eradicating the underlying structural causes of poverty. In development projects, the empowerment of individuals or groups is seen as a step towards overcoming unjust social structures and transforming political systems to be more inclusive[35]. However, one rarely finds a detailed consideration of how the empowerment of individuals or groups is supposed to lead to structural change (Cleaver, 1999: 605). One problem, commonly underestimated, concerns the motivation of individuals to participate and, after "having been empowered", fight for social change. Appeals to their social responsibilities (implying that participation in development programs and political activism are prime responsibilities) may, in practice, not serve as a convincing incentive to participate in the ways desired by development agencies (Botes/ van Rensburg, 2000: 51; Cornwell, 2002: 56f.).

Furthermore, development agencies often neglect the conflict potential inherent in true participatory and transformative development. Structural changes as envisaged, at least in theory, by many development agencies, touch upon the very foundation of a society. Those actors, who benefit from the structures in place (and who are usually also the ones in power), will hardly lean back and watch when people's movements, encouraged by outside development experts, start fighting for a "new society". Radical transformation thus poses many dangers to the people pursuing it, especially after the western "facilitators" have left the country. Moreover, it is questionable whether structural transformation can be initiated by external development agencies at all (Waddington/ Mohan, 2004: 221f.; Mansuri/ Rao, 2004: 24ff.; AGEE, 2002: 183ff.; Mohan, 2007; Cornwall, 2002: 66ff.; Bliss/ Neumann, 2006: 425).

Development bureaucracy and the nature of development: Western standards of bureaucracy are often seen as major constraints to participatory development. Critiques stress the negative impacts of rigid budget structures, short time spans for projects and inflexible deadlines for progress reports on participation (Ebrahim, 2003: 1ff.; Nolan, 1994: 376ff.). Target communities consist mostly of people who have never been exposed to such highly technical bureaucratic procedures; this often leads to elite capture when selecting individuals to cooperate with. It also limits the choice of local partner organizations. "Professional organizations" with qualified, western-oriented staff and modern offices are favored over local initiatives which may enjoy the trust and support of the people but cannot comply with the bureaucratic requirements (Platteau/ Gaspart, 2003: 1690ff.; Bliss/ Neumann, 2006: 425).

Evaluations of projects and programs are nowadays a formulaic necessity. They usually focus on measurable outputs supported by statistics instead of

---

[35] See for example
http://www.gtz.de/de/publikationen/begriffswelt-gtz/de/include.asp?lang=D&file=2_14.inc
or www.worldbank.org/empowerment (both sited on 29.10.07)

long-term outcomes, which are harder to quantify. This leads to projects being planned to satisfy the former and neglect the latter which in most cases is equally if not more important (Botes/ van Rensburg, 2000: 46f./ 50f.; Blaikie, 2006: 1952). Prevailing among many development agencies is an understanding of development as linear, intentional, one-dimensional and something which can be achieved by rational project interventions (Hickey/ Mohan[2], 2004: 15ff.). Post-development theorists, especially, expound the problems of development as predetermined and ultimate goal of all interventions. They claim that all efforts of development are inevitably top-down as the development initiators always know where the process should be heading. For them, development is a modern form of trusteeship which can never be truly participatory (Nustad, 481ff.; Dannhaeuser/ Werner, 2003: xv). Others, although being less pessimistic, acknowledge the problem of differing values and worldviews between staff from western organizations and their beneficiaries, especially with regard to empowerment projects. What to do when beneficiaries ask to be empowered in ways which are not considered empowering by western norms remains an unsolvable problem in participatory development (Cornwall, 2003: 1331; Kilby, 2006; AGEE; 2002: 180ff.; Mohan, 2007).

The five points of critique outlined in this section are among the most often cited when it comes to explaining the failure of participatory development. Many of the criticisms relate to the way development organizations function. This suggests that organizational culture may be another relevant factor when trying to account for the difficulties in successfully realizing participatory development.

3.2.5 Concluding Remarks
As demonstrated in this chapter, the participation paradigm has been dominating development debates for nearly two decades due to the many benefits expected from participatory development. Different participatory methods and approaches have been developed, ranging from those mainly concerned with questioning the beneficiaries in the planning phase of a project to those aimed at structural transformation of whole societies. In the theoretical discussion, efforts to put participation into practice, as well as the assumptions underlying the paradigm, have been criticized on several grounds. In order to deeper explore the current constraints on participatory development and elucidate under which circumstances it may be successful the following analysis focuses on the cultures and structures of development organizations.

3.3 Expounding a Link between Organizational Culture and Participation
Some authors have explicitly tried to establish a link between organizational culture and participation (Nolan, 1994; Finsterbush/ Van Wicklin, 1989: 587ff.; Chambers, 1994: 1447f.; Lloyd, 1998). These authors claim that one reason for the often unsuccessful inclusion and empowerment of beneficiaries lies in the cultures and structures of "service organizations" (see also McKnight, 1995). My M.A. thesis aims to systematically explore this assumption in the context of

development cooperation. In the debates on participation, I have identified several points which suggest that certain elements of organizational culture (as defined in section 3.1.4) are crucial to the success or failure of participatory development. I take these as a starting point for my analysis.

The first point relates to the bureaucratic culture of development agencies. Their inflexible time and budget regulations present major obstacles to successful grassroots' participation as the range of potential partners and local facilitators within the communities is reduced to a small, educated elite. A complicated bureaucracy increases the perceived distance between developers and beneficiaries which in turn complicates an equal and participatory cooperation.

Secondly, different authors suggest that the successful application of participatory methods and principles depends very much on the commitment and willingness of the individual staff member to learn and listen (e.g. Chambers, 1997: 210f.; Mansuri/ Rao, 2004: 24ff.). He/ she may be able to make a difference and influence the extent to which the development process is participatory, even if working within top-down structures set by the organization. Yet, the scope of individual influence is determined by how much participation is valued and rewarded within the organization, and by the resources (e.g. time and money) provided to realize participation. In this regard, organizational culture becomes a fruitful concept for analysis. I believe that organizations structure the behavior of their members to some extent, as I have already argued in section 3.1.4. The following example outlines how the influence of organizational culture may affect the behavior of staff with regard to participation. Development organizations often delineate their staff as "experts", who set out to help "the poor". This gives the "experts" the feeling of being superior to the project beneficiaries with whom they are to work. As a consequence, they may refuse to treat the local people as equals, show a disrespect of what they perceive as "backward", "traditional" and unscientific knowledge and demonstrate a reluctance to learn from them. All of this would, however, be necessary to realize participation.

A third relevant point in the debate on the failures of participatory development concerns the way organizations define and justify their vision and objectives. This is frequently revealed in value and mission statements. Most, if not all, development agencies follow a "development vision", which usually rests on set premises and measurable indicators defining when development has been achieved[36]. Participatory research may carry a large potential to reveal what target communities actually hope to gain from development interventions. However, when their objectives do not fit into the "value-and-procedure-catalogue" of the intervening organization, they will most likely be ignored, as demonstrated by Nauta (2006: 160ff.) in her case study of a South African NGO.

A fourth point, which is frequently made in the literature, points to the lacking abilities of development organizations to learn. Many scholars claim that the participation paradigm has not led to significant changes in the underlying structures and procedures of development cooperation. Organizations have

---

[36] A good example are the Millenium Development Goals (see Nusheler, 2005: 575ff.).

proved to be fairly slow, if not resistant, to incorporating findings from the research on participatory development, or have tried to do so by only implementing superficial corrections to their policies and strategies. The stability of organizational cultures, and the resulting inability of organizations to learn, can potentially explain why so little has changed in the international development cooperation, despite continuous criticism for more than 50 years (Nolan, 1994: 373).

These four points of discussion in the participation (and empowerment) discourse have led me to hypothesize the influence of organizational culture on participation as following:

1. The degree to which an organization has professionalized and established a formal bureaucracy may affect the relationship between the organization and its beneficiaries – a higher level of bureaucracy is expected to increase the physical and social distance between the staff and the beneficiaries.
2. The staff working in development organizations plays a crucial role in determining whether participation in programs and the empowerment of beneficiaries can be realized. However, unparticipatory structures and cultures within the organization can serve as constraining factors.
3. The values and missions of many development organizations which depict a clear, consensual and designable path to development are hard to reconcile with the more ambiguous processes which go hand in hand with true participation.
4. A failure of development organizations to learn from experience has led to the establishment of structures in development cooperation which are hard to change. This is one reason why the paradigm of participation has so far failed to produce true changes in the relations between developers and development recipients.

The following chapter further elaborates these proclaimed links by drawing on concepts from organizational and institutional theory and relating them to different case studies of development NGOs, welfare institutions and social movement organizations. This literature provides interesting insights into the effects of professionalization and bureaucratization in organizations, the role of development brokers, the functions of value-catalogues and mission statements as well as the ability of organizations to learn.

3.3.1 Professionalization and Bureaucratization
Since the late 1980s, the (development) NGO sector has witnessed an increase in professionalization. This is mainly due to growing interactions with foreign funders who saw the (financial) support of NGOs as a possibility to render the development process more democratic and participatory. In order to get access to the funds provided by foreign development agencies, NGOs had to ensure that their staff were sufficiently trained for them to be able to manage the fund-

ing, reporting, and monitoring requirements (Ebrahim, 2003: 39ff.; West, 2001: 5ff.).

As Martens (2006: 375) points out, "**[p]rofessionalization** (...) has two meanings: on one hand, it refers to the making of a profession out of a previously voluntary position and, on the other hand, it implies that staff are recruited on the basis of educational qualifications" rather than being selected for their ideological commitment to the cause of the NGO. Professionalization usually entails an increase in staff and offices, which necessitates the establishment of hierarchies in order to clearly define positions and responsibilities within the organization. In addition, procedures are standardized and job descriptions fixed to ensure that changes in staff do not obstruct the functioning of the NGO. This process is generally referred to as **bureaucratization** (Hodson, 2004: 16f.). An organization is greatly influenced by its institutional environment, which dictates how interactions between different societal actors are structured. An adaptation to these institutional structures which may be essential for the NGO to be recognized by other organizations or the state is labeled **institutionalization** (Martens, 2006: 373ff.; Lister, 2003: 178ff.; McCourt Perring, 1994: 177).

With regard to organizational culture as defined in this work, one can argue that the bureaucratization and professionalization of an organization affects its social culture as the positions and tasks of members become more formalized and the relations between staff more distant and less casual. Furthermore, one often witnesses that the material culture changes: for example, offices are renovated and dress codes changed in order to convey a more professional image.

Concerning participation, research findings suggest that professionalization may prove to be a hindrance for a NGO to live up to the expectations it was originally called for – namely, being close to the "local" population and thus being able to ensure a more participatory, decentralized development process (Murdoch, 2003: 507; Martens, 2006: 373ff.; Ebrahim, 2003: 49; Wright[2], 1994: 162f.). The "iron law of oligarchy", often cited in the literature on social movement organizations (originally developed by Michels, 1966), states that it is more or less inevitable that organizations will eventually become dominated by leadership, install a top-down bureaucracy and reposition activities to suit new demands which often divert from the original objectives of the organization (Martens, 2006: 373f.; Ostermann, 2006: 622ff.). This in turn leads to a loss of energy and commitment of members in social movement organizations (Ostermann, 2006: 622) and a loss of support from grassroots in the case of NGOs (Murdoch, 2003: 514ff.). Martens (2006: 374) cites that institutionalization often implies that "social actors... [change] their goals from working for a 'good cause' to preserving themselves". Therefore, some organizations put up great efforts to conceal their professionalization, so as to limit the perceived "distance" between them and their grassroots supporters (Edwards, 1998). Others try to legitimate their professionalization in order not to lose the trust of their beneficiaries (Murdoch, 2003: 518f.)[37].

Recent research findings suggest that neither the "iron law" nor its undesired consequences are completely inevitable but rather dependent on a number of factors. These include the characteristics of the organization's members/ staff and the motivation of its leaders (Ostermann, 2006: 625ff.). Structural factors such as the size of the organization and its dependence on external funding also present important aspects to consider when analyzing why, to what extent and with which consequences an organization has professionalized (Ostermann, 2006: 645f.; Martens, 2006: 374; Murdoch, 2003: 523ff.).

The presumed causal relationship between the degree of institutionalization and the proximity of an organization to its beneficiaries seems to work both ways. McCourt Perring (1998) demonstrates how de-institutionalization and de-professionalization were used as strategies in the UK to render in-patient hospital care more participatory, empowering and patient-oriented – albeit with mixed successes. Murdoch (2003) argues along similar lines that professionalization is a process which can be reversed if an organization feels it had to relinquish too many of its original values and ideas, especially with regard to grassroots' participation.

Organizations are confronted with a basic dilemma: in order to increase their influence, expand the scope of their activities and gain access to larger funds, they have to convincingly convey an image of being professional and efficient. Throughout this process, however, organizations often have to compromise many of the original ideals, especially with regard to participation and empowerment. Altogether, the effect of professionalization and bureaucratization on an organization's ability to initiate participatory and empowering development can be hypothesized as follows:

❖ The more professional and bureaucratic an organization is or becomes, the more difficulties it will have in establishing/ maintaining close relationships to its beneficiaries and grassroots supporters, and in rendering the development process participatory and empowering.

3.3.2 Development Brokers

As outlined in section 3.2.6, individuals, be they workers or managers, developers or beneficiaries, always act with a given system which imposes certain constraints on them – e.g. with regard to role expectations or established working

---

[37] In her case study of a feminist NGO in Columbia, Murdoch (2003) demonstrates how the formerly close relationships between the NGO staff and the women they were supporting were threatened when the NGO decided to become more professional and employ better educated and experienced staff. The NGO try to justify this decision by saying that professionalization was the only way to gain more influence and engage in policy and advocacy work on a higher level. However, by shifting its concern from practical aid to lobbing for women's rights, the NGO lost the trust and support of its former beneficiaries.

procedures (see Acre and Long, 1993: 180ff./205f.; McCourt Perring, 1994: 177; Crewe/ Harrison, 1998: 187ff.; Wright[2], 1994: 161ff.). However, researchers studying organizations and workplaces stress that work outputs and outcomes also depend very much on the individuals involved (e.g. Lloyd, 1994: 236f.). In the context of development cooperation, the importance of the individual manager, fieldworker or community leader has been repeatedly stressed – especially concerning their role of negotiating conflicting interests in and understandings of development, as well as ensuring participation (Mansuri/ Rao, 2004: 24ff.; Chambers, 1997: 210f.). Mosse/ Lewis (2006: 11ff.) speak of "development brokers", referring to those social actors who are intermediaries between the local target population of a project and the implementing development organization or between a NGO and its funders (see graphic 1).

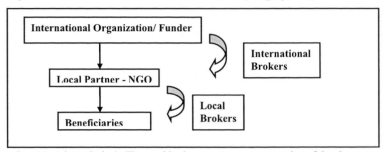

Graphic 1 (own design): The graphic shows a common conception of development cooperation: at the top there is an initiating/ funding agency which cooperates with a partner, usually some form of NGO, at the local level, where the project is to be implemented. The local NGO is often the prime implementer of the project. International staff usually facilitate the cooperation between the international and the local organization (e.g. as consultants, trainers of local staff). The local staff conveys the project to the beneficiaries who are to profit from it.

These brokers need to be able to face "both directions" and translate between the systems of the local population and the bureaucratic system of external financiers, with the aim of enabling cooperation and preventing fragmentation. In some ways the interactions between development brokers and their respective reference groups resemble patron-client relationships as demonstrated by Van Ufford (1993) and Acre/ Long (1993).

Development brokers represent the "central agents" of participatory development, as they facilitate participation on the local level – e.g. through PRA, workshops or just through being the contact persons to whom the target community can voice its concerns – and have to communicate the outcomes of these "participatory activities" to the development organization. Although they usually do not possess enough influence to guarantee that the views of the beneficiaries are really incorporated into the programs, the more skillful the brokers communicate and translate the local "voices", the more chance there is of them being heard. Caught between the conflicting interests, objectives and beliefs of the development organization and its beneficiaries, development brokers are often confronted with a dilemma: on the one hand they need to comply with the organization's culture, its rules and demands and ensure that their project plans can be realized; on the other hand they have to gain the trust of the target population in order to ensure their participation and cooperation, which sometimes requires violating or at least "bending" the rules and instructions dictated by the organization[38] (Van Ufford, 1993: 137f./144ff./155; Acre/ Long, 1993: 196ff.). To achieve both is also in the personal interests of the brokers, as they want to keep their jobs and want to be socially accepted and liked by the people they work with. If the development organization fails to incorporate the demands of the beneficiaries, the latter hold the broker accountable and he/she loses their trust. If, on the other hand, the beneficiaries refuse to accept or comply with the organization's plans, the organization will blame the broker, as it is his task to ensure local cooperation – and as a result he might lose his job.

Wright[2] (1994: 161ff.) points to the problem of the unequal power and communication resources between the agency that "employs" the broker and the recipients which have far fewer means to enforce their ideas and priorities on the project and the mediator. However, the loyalties of the development broker are not fixed; they change depending on the context. Sometimes it may be necessary to suspend the boundaries between him/herself and the beneficiaries, for example when trying to build up a relationship of trust. In other situations the broker may have to show loyalty to the "development bureaucrats", for example when he/she wants access to funds or to make use of the organization's connections to realize the demands of the beneficiaries. The position as an intermediary gives the broker some form of leverage to inflict his/her own interpretation of reality and thus control, or at least influence, outcomes and events throughout the development process (Edwards, 1994; Mosse, 2001: 160f.; Lister, 2003: 182ff.; Acre/ Long, 1993).

The behavior of the individual broker should always be interpreted with regard to the characteristics/ culture of the organization he/ she works for. Relevant factors include the degree of bureaucratization and the extent to which autonomy is granted to individual staff (Hodson, 2004: 31; McCourt Perring, 1994: 173). As Hoggett (1987: 164) states, "each layer in an organization tends to reproduce, in its dealings with the layer below, the way in which it is addressed by the layer above" (cited in Wright[2], 1994: 165).

One has to bear in mind that there is no clear cut dichotomy between developers and beneficiaries, locals and internationals or donors and recipients as some theorists (e.g. Hobart, 1993) maintain. The underlying relations of development are much more complex so that negative (or positive) development out-

---

[38] In his analysis of a development project initiated by the Dutch and the Javanese Church, Van Ufford (1993) illustrates how a "development broker" develops different strategies in order to mediate between the often irreconcilable interests of the development initiators and the village populations targeted by the project. The broker, for example, decided to ignore incompliances with the project-rules of the target groups and did not report them to his superiors in order to gain the trust of the local people and to avoid open conflicts.

comes cannot be sufficiently explained by just blaming the "self-interested de-velopment organization" or the "non-complying beneficiaries" (Crewe/ Harri-son, 1998: 177f.; Mohan, 2007). Rather, the multiplicity of actors and actions inevitably leads to unintentional and uncontrollable outcomes. Development analysts, especially with a critical stance on development, often refuse to see that there are also shared interests, identities and ideas that cut across clearly identifiable groups such as development staff and beneficiaries – for example similar goals of developers and target groups (improvement of living conditions) or personal relationships between the two sides (e.g. marriages). Sometimes for-mer beneficiaries also become developers (Crewe/ Harrison, 1998: 178ff.). These crosscutting interrelations can serve as an important starting point when trying to realize participatory development.

Obviously, there are numerous structural factors such as material differ-ences and power differences which impact on the relations between developers and beneficiaries and thus serve to separate the two groups. But focusing too much on the (more obvious) conflicts between developers and beneficiaries also misleads analysts to underestimate the differences and conflicts within each group. All in all, the following hypotheses can be drawn regarding the impact of development brokers on the successful realization of participation and empow-erment:

❖ The more skillful the broker is in translating between the implementing organization and the stakeholders at the local level, the greater are the chances that a project represents a negotiated consensus rather than a top-down enforcement.
❖ The more interrelations take place between developers and beneficiaries the easier it becomes for the broker to facilitate participation.
❖ The more compatible the culture(s) of the developers and the culture(s) of the beneficiaries are, the easier it becomes for the broker to facilitate par-ticipation.

3.3.3 Values and Mission

In order to understand how organizational culture influences participation, it is important to look at the function which organizations ascribe to having a "strong" culture. Just like big commercial enterprises, NGOs have increasingly started to develop an official value catalogue and a mission statement which one could describe as visible elements of an organization's spiritual culture. With this, they seek to, first, shape their profile for *external representation* and sec-ondly, to *internally create a common identity* to ensure smooth interactions be-tween a heterogeneous group of staff. The successful realization of the first aim depends on the extent to which the NGO can convincingly demonstrate that its programs work towards fulfilling its mission statement. The accomplishment of the second objective depends on how far the values are internalized and acted upon by staff, especially by management. Furthermore, the challenge for a NGO is to be faithful to their mission but stay flexible to adopt to new development trends at the same time (Frantz, 2005: 175ff.).

3.3.3.1 External Purpose

As NGOs are usually dependent on external funding – either from large international development agencies or from private sponsors – they primarily model their values and mission to fit the interests and views of their funders (Van Ufford, 1993: 142). This usually requires portraying the NGO as helping people who are poor, helpless and have problems which they cannot solve without external support (Crewe/ Harrison, 1998: 191f.)[39]. On the local level, however, the NGO may be confronted with people who are by no means helpless, but have clear ideas on what their problems are and how these could be solved, although they might need external support to realize these solutions (Acre/ Long, 1993: 188ff.). Nauta (2006), who ethnographically studied a development NGO in South Africa, demonstrates how the NGO tried to "translate" the realities it found at the local (project) level to fit its original program plans and to reinforce the (external) image of the NGO by applying three different strategies: First, research, which was designed to legitimate the NGO's programmatic, strategic and activist approaches.[40] Secondly, "participatory" workshops, in which the NGO set the agenda and strategically conceptualized the encounter with the beneficiaries to attain the results it wanted – namely the agreement of the beneficiaries on the interventions planned. And thirdly, reports, in which the NGO presented "their version of reality" and which it then used to justify their developmental (and political) aims (Nauta, 2006: 164ff.).

The problems described above (obviously) present an obstacle for realizing participatory and empowering development as the latter relies, to a large extent, on mutual respect and cooperation on equal terms between the NGO and its beneficiaries. Not only does the NGO need to take the views and ideas of its beneficiaries into account, but it also has to be regarded as a trustworthy and legitimate partner. As Lister (2003: 182) states "[n]ormative and cognitive legitimacy is based on congruence between the ideals and 'mental models' of the stakeholders and the agency (Not just 'Do we agree with the vision of this agency?' but 'Is this agency 'one of us'?')." This implies that the values and mission of the NGO must not only suit the aspiration of its funders, but also that

---

[39] In their study of shelters for runaways and young homeless in Britain, Hutson and Liddiard (1993) found that the way a welfare agency defined their clients had a large effect on what „solutions" he/ she was offered. Similar problems of clients were interpreted completely differently depending on which agency was questioned. The authors conclude that „… the viewpoint prevailing in a project will depend on its history, the basis on which its funds are sought and its basic political and social aims" (ibid: 43). The same is probably true for development organizations.

[40] The danger that organizations instrumentalize research for their purposes puts the researcher who has been employed by the organization in an ambivalent position. He/ she is confronted with the difficulty of combining critical analysis with the interest of the organization as depicted by Mosse (2001) and Mosse/ Lewis (2006: 2ff.).

of its beneficiaries in order to pave the way for a successful and participatory cooperation.

Faith-based NGOs (FBOs) try to achieve this by appealing to a religious ideology and basing their programs and approaches on religious values. Often, the funders of FBOs (which usually consist at least to some extent of religious institutions, e.g. churches) as well as the beneficiaries (although this is not a necessity) share a similar faith. Thus, religion has the potential to produce a common identity between the various development stakeholders, which disguises other (cultural, material or social) differences (Frantz, 2005: 179/ 193ff.; Osterman, 2006: 646f.)[41].

3.3.3.2 Internal Purpose

Organizations can "acquire a life and momentum independent of the people who make them up" (Hirsch/ Gellner, 2001: 12; see also Douglas, 1987) and thus need "disciplining". As Hirsch/ Gellner (ibid) ascertain "much organizational time and effort goes into controlling and disciplining those on the inside. These controls can be both subtle and complex". In order for an organization to function efficiently, internal differences between staff need to be kept to a minimum – Frantz (2005: 189ff.) speaks of "diversity management" - which requires creating common understandings and identities. This is achieved through symbols, myths, socialization, rites and also by developing a value-catalogue and a mission statement (Beyer/ Trice, 1988: 141f.) which Schein (2004: 225f.) refers to as the creation of organizational culture. The creation of a common identity does not only serve to limit conflicts, but also to motivate the staff to work together for a shared aim. This aim, and especially the strategies on how to achieve it, can reveal the importance ascribed to participation by the organization.

One type of conflict, frequently cited in the literature on social organizations (e.g. Frantz, 2005: 177f.; Aare, 1998), arises over the issue of *how* to achieve social development. Often, this work-related dissension is fought between two distinctive groups which Frantz (2005: 177f.) has labeled "ideologists" and "technocrats". Whereas the ideologists are attracted to working in development cooperation because of a desire to "help" without necessarily having any specific qualifications in the field of development, the technocrats are explicitly trained for development work (usually they have a relevant university degree) and are more "professional" in their approach to development. The former usually take a less strategic approach to development and do not or only superficially consider issues, which are not directly related to "helping the beneficiaries" (such as financial management, legal issues, accountability towards donors, research and evaluation etc.). The technocrats, on the other side, insist on getting all the formalities right, but sometimes forget the real issue at hand; namely, the people who are to benefit. The conflict between ideologists and technocrats often correlates with intergenerational divergences, whereas the latter are represented by younger generations of university graduates who have entered the field of development cooperation in the last one or two decades. The

---

[41] For a more detailed analysis of FBOs see Krige (2007).

approach an organization takes to achieve its objectives depends largely on which of the two factions has gained the upper hand and may at times be contested (Aare, 1998: 59ff.).

Usually, however, an organization will clearly indicate its position on issues which could potentially lead to conflicts among staff. One way to do this is to establish value and mission statements. Once established, they will not only prevent open arguments among staff on issues which are settled in these statements (for example on what approach an organization adopts). They will also play an important role with regard to the selection of staff, as they provide a first indicator (for the NGO as well as for the staff) as to whether the ideas of the organization and a new staff/ applicant are congruent. This is especially evident in FBOs, where applicants who cannot convincingly demonstrate a commitment to the religious values of the organization have few chances of being employed (Frantz, 2005: 181/ 193ff.).

How does this now relate to participation? In brief, one can say that some values and missions are more compatible with participation then others. An organization which is primarily concerned with technological issues and/ or which presents itself more as a business enterprise than a social organization will probably go differently about participation than an organization which emphasizes its commitment to "soft factors" such as partnership, solidarity and intercultural understanding. In sum, values and mission statements are indicators of the kind of approach an organization adopts in order to achieve social development. They will, explicitly or implicitly, also hint at an organization's standpoint on participation and thus attract people who concur with these values.

As shown in the preceding two sections (3.3.3.1 and 3.3.3.2), the values and the mission statements give an image to an organization which affects how it is regarded by its beneficiaries. Furthermore, these elements of the organizational culture serve to clarify the goals and procedures of the organization in order to reduce conflicts and also motivate the staff to work for a common aim. New staff members are selected on the basis of how well they can identify themselves with the values and mission. With regard to participation and empowerment, the effect of the values and the mission statement of an NGO can be hypothesized as following:

❖ If these values and mission statements are only designed to suit funders, they may not be congruent with the beneficiaries' culture(s) and thus present an obstacle to participation.

❖ If the mission of an organization is to send out professional experts to help "people with deficiencies and problems" rather than to work in partnership and provide support for the beneficiaries to realize their own "solutions", it will unlikely follow a participatory and empowering development approach. If the values of an organization center on mutual respect, partnership and cooperation, rather than primarily on technological and business-related factors, they demonstrate an organization's commitment to participation and empowerment.

❖ The way an organization presents itself is an indicator of what kind of people (will) work for the organization – the more an organization portrays itself as a professional and technocratic business enterprise, the less likely it becomes that people who are committed to "soft factors" such as participation and empowerment will choose to work for the organization or will be employed by the organization.

3.3.4 Organizational Learning and Change

As stated above, the participation paradigm has not led to significant changes in the international development system because development organizations have been hesitant to alter their structures and working procedures or, in other words, have demonstrated an inability to learn. The concept of organizational learning was developed and gained influence in the late 1970s (Argyris/ Schön, 1996: xvii). Today, many organizational researchers refer to the concept, and it is very prominent also in the popular science (see for example Senge, 1990). The main controversy with regard to organizational learning concerns whether learning occurs as an intentional and thus manageable process (e.g. Senge, 1990: 10; Schein, 2004: 319ff.), or whether change in organizations depends on a multiplicity of factors and influences and is therefore (to some extent) unintentional and uncontrollable (e.g. Ebrahim, 2003: 107; McCourt Perring, 1994: 177f.; Nauta, 2006: 154f.)[42].

Researchers have proposed different ideas of how learning in organizations takes place. Two influential concepts, well summarized by Ebrahim (2003: 108ff.), stem from March (1999) and Argyris/ Schön (1996). March (1999: 5ff./ 75ff.) discerns three types of learning: *Learning by doing* refers to improvements through routine in a stable environment. *Learning by exploring* implies taking risks, experimenting and taking on new, innovative approaches. And *Learning by imitating* entails the diffusion of technologies and information from one organization to another, for example through staff transfer or cooperation between organizations. Argyris and Schön (1996: 20ff.) differentiate between two levels of learning: single loop and double loop, whereby the former denotes an improvement in work efficiency (on the program level) and the latter involves a modification of underlying norms and values.

Ebrahim (2003: 110ff.) has singled out three governing factors which can either enable or constrain learning: first, the cognitive and practical capacities of individuals (and the organization as a whole). Secondly, the power relationships *between* organizations – e.g. with reference to the exchange of resources (money) or coalition-building (networks) – and *within* organizations – concerning e.g. conflicts between subcultures, internal hierarchies and coalitions. The third and most important factor affecting organizational learning relates to perceptual frames and worldviews (part of the organizational culture) which are

---

[42] For a general summary of this discussion see Martin et al. (2004: 9/15/17); Argyris/ Schön (1996: xix); March (1999: 7f.).

products of history and environmental stimuli and underlie individual and organizational action. As Ebrahim (2003: 113) states

"[p]erceptual frames are not simply one of many variables affecting learning – they are the basic infrastructure through which situations are organized, defined and given meaning. These frames can constrain learning by structuring or guiding how (and what) problems are perceived, what sort of information is collected, and how that information is analyzed and interpreted."

It is well documented (e.g. by McCourt Perring: 1994; Ebrahim, 2003: 50f.; Schein, 2004: 225f.) that norms, ideas and rules which guided the initial development of an organization have a long-lasting impact on future developments within that organization[43].

Who restrains/ shapes organizational learning and structural change comprises an important question – especially in the literature on development NGOs. The author of this work agrees with Crewe/ Harrison (1998: 176) and Friedman (2006: 204), who state that it is wrong to assume that change is only driven by western developers, as this does not acknowledge the multiplicity of resistances and unintentional outcomes of development caused by the actions of different stakeholders, including the beneficiaries. Ebrahim (2003: 1ff.) asserts that both NGOs and their funders hold some kind of power leverage: while NGOs need money and have to comply with the conditions of funders, funders need a good reputation. This depends on reports by the NGOs which portray successful outcomes of the interventions sponsored. Ebrahim (ibid) shows how this mutual dependence leads to a cooperation between NGOs and funders, which often impedes learning and structural change within the field of development. Successive failures (or refusals) of development agencies to change the factors which caused unsuccessful outcomes in their projects lead Nauta (2006: 168) and Nolan (1994) to generally question the idea that these organizations are learning organizations. Van Ufford (1993) demonstrates how development organizations make use of a "strategy of ignorance" and "filter and package" information (Mosse, 2001: 164) in order to prevent learning, which would force them to alter their programs (see also Acre/ Long, 1993: 186f.).

However, Ebrahim (2003: 41ff.) also acknowledges significant mechanisms for change in development organizations – from top to bottom as well as from bottom to top. Top-down learning occurs through the transfer of knowledge by "development experts" and through conditionality, for example when NGOs are forced to implement current development trends such as Gender, Participation etc. into their programs. Bottom-up learning (from local to national and international levels) can happen when former local NGO staff become consultants in large development agencies, or when experiences from NGOs are spread through networks to other NGOs and networks. Ebrahim (2003: 45ff.) believes that participatory methods such as PRA and exchange programs be-

---

[43] In institutional theory this phenomenon is referred to as path dependency (Hall/ Taylor, 1996: 9f.).

tween local and international development practitioners also present opportunities for bottom-up change.

The following hypotheses come to reflect the relationship between an organization's ability to learn and the extent to which it will commit itself to participatory and empowering development:

- ❖ The less the original (founding) values, concepts and approaches of an organization are focused on participation and empowerment, the less likely it is that the organization will promote "true" participatory and empowering development, also in the long run.
- ❖ The more an organization is endowed with mechanisms to change and/ or possesses structural features that allow for learning and change, the higher are the chances that the organization can react to (new) trends in development cooperation (e.g. participation), integrate new research findings and alter its underlying concepts. (If this is not the case, an organization which has formerly followed a top-down development approach will not likely be able to successfully instigate participatory development).

3.4 Concluding Remarks

The assumptions outlined in sections 3.2.6 and 3.3 seem to have some analytical potential, as they correlate with findings from organizational analysts and ethnographers. Furthermore, they can be linked to concepts and models which have been developed in institutional/ organizational theory. Therefore, the influence of organizational culture on participation and empowerment of beneficiaries can be modeled as follows:

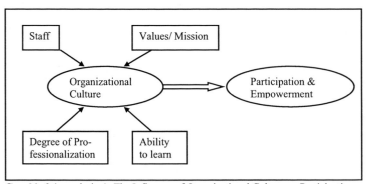

Graphic 2 (own design): The Influence of Organizational Culture on Participation

The second part of this M.A. thesis is designed to further explore the links between organizational culture and participation by applying the concepts introduced above to an empirical example – a social organization in Pretoria.

39

4. The Tshwane Leadership Foundation – A Case Study

The following chapter is based on the empirical data I collected during three months of fieldwork in the inner city of Pretoria and the greater Metropolitan area - Tshwane[44]. In the first section (4.1), I briefly introduce the Tshwane Leadership Foundation (TLF) and the setting it operates in. In the following I expand on the organizational culture (section 4.2) as well as the operational approach (section 4.3) of the organization. Section 4.4 consists of a comprehensive analysis of the concepts and hypotheses developed in section 3.3, which are applied to the case of TLF. Finally, in section 4.5, I briefly reflect on the inferences which can be drawn from the case study for the field of development cooperation in general.

4.1 Presentation of TLF

It is difficult to classify TLF as an organization. To give the reader a general impression, however, the following attempt of categorization may suffice: first and foremost, TLF is a faith-based organization with a strong developmental focus. TLF aspires (but has not yet achieved) to become a broad civil society movement in the long run[45].

4.1.1 History

The idea to set up an ecumenical community organization in Pretoria was developed in 1992 with the aim of reacting to the massive changes taking place in the inner city as the apartheid was coming to end. Six different churches came together and in 1993 created the Pretoria Community Ministries (PCM). Within 18 months, they worked out a constitution and in 1994 PCM officially registered as a legally constituted Charity Trust (Krige, 2007: 69ff.; INT: 2). In April 1993, the first project – The Potter's House, a shelter for women – had been opened and run by six volunteers who were dedicated to the cause of PCM. In the following years, PCM started to engage in various sectors of inner city community work, and as the organization grew, more and more projects were created. Krige (2007: 70) describes the years between 1993 and 2003 as the "pioneering phase" of PCM's institutional development (a brief chronology can be found on the TLF website).

In 2003, a new era started as the Tshwane Leadership Foundation (TLF) was established with the intention of forming and strengthening a multi-facetted movement of communities, programs and institutions. PCM was integrated into TLF and, up until today, represents the "pillar" for social development.

---

[44] The City of Tshwane Metropolitan Municipality (CTMM) was newly founded on December 5th, 2000 and includes various municipalities and councils which had previously served the greater Pretoria and surrounding areas. It has a population of approximately 2.2 million people and covers an area of 3200km². The name Pretoria today only refers to one centrally located area within the CTMM. The inner city where TLF is mainly involved is still referred to as Pretoria. The name Tshwane literally translates to "we are all the same" in the Tswana language (http://www.tshwane.gov.za/).
[45] For a good discussion of the distinctive characteristics of faith-based organizations and the role they (can) play in development see Krige, 2007; Kruip, 2007 and Mkhatsha, 2007.

4.1.2 Current Structure and Programs

Since 2003, five pillars – Social Development, Arts Development, Social Housing, Capacity Building and Economic Development – each consisting of different programs and institutions, are managed under the TLF superstructure. Some of the programs have grown out of the work of TLF and today constitute independent legal entities, which are still closely affiliated to the Foundation (see graphic 3).

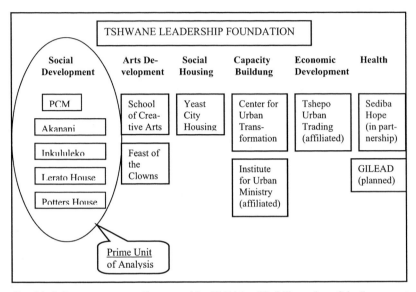

Graphic 3: Programs managed/ supported by TLF (simplified illustration of the "movement tree" found on the TLF website)

Starting with 6 volunteers in 1993, TLF today employs 83 staff members. This represents an annual growth rate of 17.5 percent. 85.5 percent of the staff is black and 75.9 percent are women (staff list, July 11th, 2007). The TLF management team consists of eight people, of whom four are black and five are female (information obtained from TLF website). In addition to the paid staff, TLF is supported by international volunteers, approximately ten at a time, and an always changing number of local volunteers. The international volunteers usually stay for a period between three and twelve months and mainly come from Germany.

TLF operates under the supervision of a Board of Trustees, which is comprised of twelve to 16 members. These come from the partner churches, associate churches or from organizations which emerged out of PCM. The board appoints the managing director of TLF. Furthermore, it has to approve financial and programmatic strategies of TLF. The management team consists of the directors of TLF and PCM, the program coordinators and a co-opted member. It meets bi-weekly to deal with operational issues. The programs which are affiliated to TLF or managed in partnership have their own management structures, but are supported by TLF in their operations (information obtained from TLF website).

In 2006/ 2007, TLF had a budget of 4.2 million Rand[46] (Krige, 2007: 78). The organization is supported by three types of funders: the government, international donors (among them, for example, the European Union, the International Labor Organization and the German Ministry of Economic Cooperation and Development (BMZ)) and a variety of South African funders including churches, companies and individuals. Each group of funders contributes roughly a third to the budget (II: 05.07.07; INT: 2).

I have chosen PCM as the core unit of my analysis (see graphic 3). PCM is made up of four programs or ministries: The *Potters House*, which is a shelter for women; *Lerato House*, which is a shelter for girls; *Akanani*, which is divided into a street center for homeless people and a hospiz accommodating terminally ill homeless people; and *Inkululeko*, which is a community center for people from the economically marginalized community of Salvokop, including a day care center for children from low-income families. PCM has its own management, which is basically comprised of one manager and four coordinators (one for each project) and takes most decisions relating to the operation of the projects. The initiation of new programs as well as the annual budget, however, has to be approved by the TLF management and the TLF board (INT: 2).

I decided to lay my prime focus on PCM for the following reasons: first, PCM encompasses all the social development projects of TLF, which are of greatest relevance to my research questions. In these projects, the participation and empowerment approach of the organization and the relationships between staff and beneficiaries are best observable. Secondly, PCM represents the founding constituent of TLF and therefore has the longest history of institutional development. It is also the largest "pillar" of TLF in terms of staff and facilities. Thirdly, I have conducted participant observation as a volunteer for Lerato House and most of the people I interacted with on a daily basis also worked for one of the PCM projects.

In the following case study, I will relate the insights, which stem largely from my "PCM experience", to TLF as a whole. The most important reason for this is that TLF views itself as one coherent movement and community; the most significant events and rites, for example, are celebrated together with all staff. Furthermore, the vision and mission of the organization can only be understood by looking at TLF as a whole, as each pillar fulfills a special part in achieving TLF's overall objectives (see section 2.1; TLF Blue File; TLF Information Flyer).

---

[46] This equals a sum of approximately 420.000 Euro.

4.1.3 Social and Institutional Setting[47]

Most of TLF's programs are located in the inner city, although there are also programs that extend to the Greater Tshwane Metropolitan Area.

Since the end of the apartheid in 1994, dramatic changes have taken place in the inner city. Many black people who had been confined to their townships under apartheid legislation moved into the formerly "white" city center which, for decades, had been the "heartland of Afrikaner history" (Krige, 2007: 65). This, consecutively, led not only to an exodus of the white (and wealthy) former residents to the suburbs, but also to the "flight" of businesses and investors (ibid). Today, Tshwane's city center no longer resembles a "western" capital, but is characterized by countless street hawkers and bustling markets which reflect a more "African" lifestyle. Cheap outlets and fast food places, decaying buildings, a dysfunctional infrastructure and the huge informal economy reflect the growing poverty which in turn nourishes drug dealing, prostitution, xenophobia and an unreasonably high crime rate. Tshwane is the South African city with the second highest rate of violent crime, surpassed only by Johannesburg. The crime rate has increased dramatically since 1994 (Schönteich/ Louw, 2001). Most if not all of the (permanent) TLF staff members have been robbed, attacked, menaced and/ or harassed at some point in their life. Some of the programs (such as the street and bad building outreach) are temporarily inoperative due to safety precautions. Many of the beneficiaries have been victims of rape, physical abuse and/ or trafficking (II: 11.07.; 26.07.; 13.08.; 24.08.; 05.09.; 11.09.). The black and white divide in Pretoria manifests itself not only in settlement patterns (white suburbs and gated communities, black city center and former townships) but plays a role in all aspects of life to an extent that seems inconceivable and at times unbearable, especially to foreigners (II: 04.07.; 11.07.; 01.08.; O: 20.07.; 14.09.)[48].

TLF operates within in a diverse institutional setting. With the aim of "working (…) for urban transformation" (TLF Information Flyer), it has partnered with the city council, public service providers (police, hospitals etc.), churches, universities, as well as several local and national organizations. The collaboration with the City Council presents the most important, but also the most contested and difficult form of cooperation. On the one hand, TLF wants to gain influence in the city, hold the local government accountable to fulfill its social responsibilities and work together to achieve more comprehensive results. On the other hand, TLF wants to remain an independent organization and body of control which is able to present an opposition to the government sector, and

---

[47] In this section I focus on the local context in which TLF operates. I do not comment on the overall situation in South Africa. A good summary of the political, economic, social and socio-cultural conditions in South Africa can be found in SLE, 2003: 19-29.

[48] The black and white issue also affects the working relations within TLF although this is not always overtly revealed. The following quote from an interviewee presents a good example of how individuals secretly brood over the problem: "things have obviously changed (…), have they changed because (…) there is only black staff left? Would it have changed the same direction if they [the white staff] were still part of this? Would it change differently if they come? (…) I always ask myself that" (INT: 3).

fears being co-opted when working too closely with the "power crazy" (INT: 4) City Council[49] (INT: 2,3,6; O: 01.08.).

4.2 Organizational Culture

The management of TLF puts a lot of time and effort in contemplating the organization's culture, and tries to intentionally "shape" it. This is especially evident with regard to the spiritual and material aspects, as I will point out in the following sections 4.2.1 and 4.2.3. However, as has been elucidated in section 3.1, many facets of an organization's culture cannot be deliberately created and remain beyond the control of the management, especially those relating to the relations among staff or between staff and beneficiaries. I reflect on these more ambiguous (social) aspects of TLF's organizational culture in section 4.2.2.

4.2.1 Spiritual Aspects
4.2.1.1 Important Rituals

The spiritual components are the best discernible aspects of TLF's organizational culture. They serve not only to define the "moral" standpoint of the organization, but also to convey this standpoint to staff (and beneficiaries) and clarify what is expected of the individual when he/she wants to be an accepted member of TLF. In this regard, rituals fulfill a central function, and I will thus reflect on them in more detail. One can differentiate between weekly, monthly and annual rituals.

The most important ritual is the **weekly devotion**, which takes place every Friday morning between 8.00 and 11.00 o'clock, and is obligatory for staff. The devotion is held by the managing director of TLF, a theologian. In addition to fulfilling a religious purpose, it aims to unite, motivate and encourage the staff (INT: 7). Positive accomplishments and successes as well as birthdays of individual members are celebrated, and new staff is welcomed. Everyone also has the opportunity to share negative experiences and personal problems. Support is then provided in the form of collective prayers. In group sessions, usually following a lecture by the director, the employees discuss, define and reflect on values, visions and other elements of the TLF's culture. These sessions intend to reveal the opinion of staff, for example, on how TLF can become a coherent and dedicated movement (O: 14.09.), which function and importance is attributed to TLF being a community (O: 13.07.; 17.08.), or whether staff considers TLF rituals as liberating or as oppressing (O: 20.07.). The director also uses his sermon to voice concerns about problematic developments within TLF, to urge

---

[49] The ambivalence of wanting to cooperate with the City Council but at the same time fearing to be "co-opted" was especially evident with regard to the Feast of the Clowns. This TLF event aims to celebrate the diversity of the city but at the same time create awareness of current problems. In 2007, TLF organized the Feast together with the City Council for the first time, a major benefit being that for the first time the budget for the Feast was balanced. However, there was great skepticism among the TLF staff as to whether the aspect of criticizing negative developments (including political setbacks) in the city would be challenged by the City Council (O: 03.08.; INT: 6).

staff to be more committed, or to talk about conflicts within the organization (O: 20.07.; 17.08.; 14.09.).

The **TLF retreat,** which takes place twice a year, constitutes another important ritual. Although its main function concerns the planning and evaluation of TLF's programs (INT: 2; O: 06.07.), the reflection of TLF's organizational culture (similar to that in the weekly devotions) also presents a significant component. During the mid-year retreat, a whole day was devoted to discussing topics such as chances and difficulties of leadership in TLF, uniting and dividing elements of the organization's culture as well as future challenges (O: 07.07.).

Another prominent ritual is the **Feast of the Clowns,** which has taken place annually since the year 2000, with the aim of celebrating the city but also making aware of current problems. During a week in August, TLF organizes and invites staff, beneficiaries and other stakeholders to different workshops and theatre shows. The highlight of the week is a street festival with craft and food stalls, music and cultural performances as well as games and fun activities for children. The event also includes a march through the inner city of Pretoria. Each year, a different theme is chosen for the Feast – in 2007 it was "Taking back our Streets" - to which all the activities should somehow refer (O: 20.-26.08.; 31.08.; INT: 7).

The **monthly celebration** is a ritual aspiring to strengthen the relationships between beneficiaries and staff. It is organized by a different TLF ministry each month and includes an evening program (e.g. speeches, poetry and song presentations) and a shared supper (O: 26.07.).

TLF performs many other rituals, most of which strive to create a feeling of community, spread and consolidate the (religious) values of TLF and to reward, motivate and encourage the staff and/ or beneficiaries. Singing and common meals – key elements of nearly all rituals - are especially enjoyed and appreciated by the participants (O: 06.07.; 07.07.; 09.07.; 15.09.; II: 17.07.; INT: 6). Furthermore, rituals help the staff to cope with the many problems they face every day and provide a space to express their frustration and despair. Hence, rituals often encompass very emotional moments (O: 07.07.; 17.08.; 17.09.). However, the rituals do not always succeed in achieving the desired impact and are often experienced very differently. Whereas, for example, for some staff members the weekly devotions are an occasion to get new strength and energy, for others they present an annoying obligation, which keeps them from doing their work (II: 13.07.; 19.07.; O: 20.07.). In practice, the behavior of staff and management sometimes deviates extremely from what is preached in the rituals and some rituals have over time faded to become regular events that no longer serve their actual purpose, but are performed out of habit (O: 07.09.; 24.08.; 14.09.). This again demonstrates that a dominant organizational culture can, to some extent, be established (for example through certain rituals), but that it cannot be completely enforced and always remains somewhat erratic.

Other elements of spiritual culture such as symbols, myths and legends, also prevail within TLF, but due to spatial limitations I will not analyze these in detail. Symbols, for example the cross in the emblem of TLF, often reflect the

Christian background of the organization. Myths and legends often relate to the founding years of the organization, where specific individuals overcame incredible hardships to create what TLF is today (INT: 2, 7; II: 05.07.; 26.07.).

4.2.1.2 Vision, Mission and Values[50]

TLF is a vision-oriented organization, aspiring to "see whole, restored and empowered communities where people flourish in God's presence". The mission it follows is to "work in partnership with churches and communities for urban transformation" which entails "[v]isioning, incubating, capacitating, advocating, and resourcing" (Krige, 2007: 72).

When looking at TLF's objectives, one can differentiate between three strategies and aims, summarized in the following table.

OBJECTIVE/ AIM	STRATEGY/ APPROACH[51]
Help poor and vulnerable people, and create communities which develop capable leaders, have access to resources such as housing, employment, education etc. and can handle their own problems	Community Development
Develop the city, facilitate intercultural communication and a respectful interaction between people of different race, gender, faith and class and promote the idea of partnerships between all relevant stakeholders	Institutional Development and collective Empowerment/ (Structural change)
Spread Christian values and messages	Missionary Work

Table 2: TLF Objectives and Strategies

In the style of other Leadership Foundations[52], TLF has developed a comprehensive set of values – 17 in total - to which every staff member (and to some extent also the beneficiaries) should submit. One can classify four types of values whereby the boundaries between them are fluent and some fit in more than one category:

1. **Religious (Christian) values**, for example "[w]e value God's total redemption in Jesus Christ" or "[w]e value biblical principles".
2. **Values** related to the **city** and the **communities**, such as "[w]e value the city as a place where needs and resources meet" and "[w]e value community as a place of intimacy".
3. **Values** relating to **moral principles** including justice, truth and reconciliation.

---

[50] The Vision, Mission, Values and Objectives as well as the TLF Policy are all explicated in the TLF Blue File, the TLF information flyer or the TLF website.

[51] The strategies mentioned in this table (with the exclusion of "Missionary Work") refer to the development approaches and strategies mentioned in Table 1. The designations are based on my interpretation of the TLF programs.

[52] The Leadership Foundation model was developed in the USA and has, since the 1990s, expanded to a small number of cities around the world (Krige, 2007: 34ff.). It underlies TLF's structure and conceptual framework.

4. **Values** which more concretely address the **expected conduct of staff**, for example "[w]e value a simple life-style" or [w]e value servant leadership which is committed to the city and in solidarity with the marginalized".

In one of his speeches at the mid-year retreat, the TLF managing director suggested that these values are the "glue" which holds the organization together and illustrated this idea in the adjacent graphic 4 (O: 07.07.).

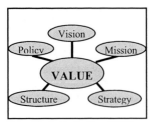

Graphic 4: Centrality of TLF Values

The TLF values "are intended to be part of a 24/7 lifestyle" (Krige, 2007: 72), which means they should also be adhered to by staff outside of the immediate working context. The implicit idea is for TLF affiliates to set a good example as they are working in a milieu where moral and social values have deteriorated severely and in which hostility, violence, and irreverence prevail (INT: 7). The values also emphasize that TLF considers itself as a community and family of which one is either fully a part with all the ensuing obligations, or not at all. Most of the values, especially those relating to moral principles and those addressing the conduct of staff, are taken up and further specified in the TLF Policy. Violations by staff are criticized and may be sanctioned (INT: 2; O: 14.09.; 19.09.). As one informant put it:

"[W]e are a community and there are consequences to that…, apart from being a community, we are Christians, we are faith-based, so we have to have high moral standards, it's like the national cricket team you are representing your country, so what you do, you can't embarrass the place and then the name of this whole organization goes down because someone takes drugs, or gets drunk every weekend or whatever, there is definitely limits to that, but we realized that we can monitor these things individually, the stories always come out and then people will be talked to and then there will be discussions saying 'well, this is your private life, but there are limits' " (INT: 2).

Regarding the Christian values of TLF, the staff is expected to respect and be open-minded towards them, however no one is forced (how) to believe. The absolute majority of staff does have a Christian background but, due to coming from different congregations, everyone practices his/ her religion differently and does not necessarily share a common view on what it means to be a Christian. Although being a Christian is in most cases an important criterion for employment, there are exceptions: the volunteers coming from Germany, for example, sometimes do not have a religious background (INT: 2, 3, 7).

Despite the fairly rigorous moral principles, those beneficiaries and (prospective) employees who have difficulties in living according to TLF values (e.g. drug and alcohol addicts, prostitutes) are respected and taken into the community, given that they demonstrate a willingness to learn and try to alter their way of life. Staff and beneficiaries who break the rules are always given second (and often a third, fourth and fifth) chance to rehabilitate themselves. This attitude reflects the belief in the importance of forgiveness and also the conviction that every individual can change for the better (INT: 4, 3; O: 20.08.; 03.09.; II: 12.09.). All in all, the vision, mission and values of TLF serve as important guidelines and an orientation for staff (and beneficiaries) on what is expected of them as members of the community. Although they have been primarily defined by the management, staff is given the opportunity to voice their opinion on whether they believe the guidelines to be adequate – for example during devotions or the retreats (O: 07.07.; 20.07.). If the guidelines are not or no longer supported by the majority of staff, they may be revised. Thus, the vision, mission and values are not static, but they portray an important indicator of the present-day organizational culture of TLF. The relevance of the TLF values and mission regarding participation and empowerment statement will be analyzed in section 4.4.3.

4.2.2 Social Aspects
4.2.2.1 Staff
Diversity is a central characteristic of TLF. The staff members come from 14 different denominations, speak eleven different languages and comprise a variety of nationalities (II: 05.07.). They are united by the idea of constituting not only a workforce but a community. This entails that everyone can and even is expected to share personal problems as well as success stories. A dedication to mutual care, which is expressed by praying for each other during Friday devotions, prevails among TLF staff and supersedes the barriers of race, gender, language or position. Hierarchies exist only with regard to work-related decisions and tasks but, at least in theory, should not play a role in personal interactions.

On many different occasion people stressed that working for TLF is more than an ordinary profession, and, for them, signifies a passion and a calling (INT: 1, 4, 5, 6, 7; II: 12.07.). Therefore, it is generally considered to be more important for a staff member to show commitment and a belief in the value of community than to have sophisticated (technical) qualifications (INT: 5). When asked about the criteria for staff selection, two PCM coordinators answered the following:

"We don't actually stick on what they have acquired educationally, but we really look at are these people called, the calling, are they passionate about working with the community that is disadvantaged and marginalized, that is the first thing that we actually look at, and then of course we look at their experience and their skills but the most important thing is their calling, their passion" (INT: 6)

"I want someone that, even if someone hasn't bathed for two weeks, to be there and stand with them, just to be there, walk an extra mile, those for me are the right kind of people, they may have all sorts of skills and education but at the end of the day you need to have a heart for these kind of people, cause we need to be there as facilitators, as catalysts" (INT: 4).

Notwithstanding all the benefits, the "community approach" also has its downsides. It entails, for example, that the staff is required to devote a lot of time and energy to TLF even outside official working hours – for community events organized by TLF, in cases of emergency, when taking care of a sick colleague or a beneficiary who needs special attention. Therefore, many employees expressed

48

feeling overworked, burned out, and not being able to cope with their obligations (INT: 3, 5; II: 25.07; 27.08. 16.08.; O: 23.07.; 17.09.).

Furthermore, several of the staff members suffer from emotional stress
and related illnesses (O/ II: 16.07; 26.07.; 31.07.; 06.08.; 14.08.; 11.09.). The
TLF community approach does not adhere to the concept of professional distance, usually practiced in social work (INT: 7). As a consequence, one cannot
distance oneself from the often severe problems of the beneficiaries (and colleagues) as everyone is regarded as part of the community and deserves care and
compassion. Many of the staff members come from difficult social backgrounds
themselves – a large number of them have formerly been TLF *beneficiaries* –
which further aggravates the problem (INT: 5; II: 12.07; 26.07.; 20.08.). Moreover, the work itself is often challenging and frustrating. Recurrently, staff
members question the impact of their work and query whether their efforts actually make a difference, although there are, of course, also success stories which
bring about rewarding and euphoric moments (II: 12.07.; 20.07.; 01.08.; 06.08.;
03.09.; 17.09.). The following quotation from an interviewee, who was asked
whether she is content with her work, demonstrates the ambivalences related to
being a TLF employee:

"[T]hat is a very heavy questions [laughs], you know I am happy that I am working and I am
working according to my call, I think this is what I am supposed to be doing, but it really is a
very hard job, so it is not like you would be 'happy happy', it is always difficult, cause we
always have difficult kinds of people, it is women who are busy with drugs, you have to try to
change these women who don't really want to change sometimes (…) Then I have to work
day and night, and at the end of the day I haven't done anything of my list, and everything is
urgent, (…) it is really too much, it becomes too much, again it is because we are short of
staff, cause I cannot delegate other people to do it because we don't have enough staff, but
still there is too much to do" (INT: 5).

The difficult working conditions, combined with the high expectations of TLF
regarding commitment to the community and the comparatively low salaries[53],
lead to a high staff turnover. They also create major difficulties for finding new
employees, especially in those positions which require trained and experienced
personal, as most qualified people on the job market are not willing to work for
the TLF salary (INT: 3; II/ O: 20.07.; 16.08.; 10.09.). Therefore, central posts
(such as the IT administrator and even a coordinator post) have, in the past, been
filled with (international) volunteers as they possess at least some of the technical skills required (for example computer or driving skills) and do not receive a
salary (INT: 5, 6, 7; O: 30.08.). The problem of finding and keeping qualified
staff will be further explicated in the section 4.4.1 on professionalisation and
bureaucratization below.

---

[53] The point that TLF salaries were low when compared with other employers in the social
sector (especially the government) was repeatedly mentioned to me. I did not, however, obtain concrete figures on the salaries paid by TLF. According to Krige (2007: 102), these range
between 1.500 and 12.500 Rand, depending on the position and the type of job. As of November 2007, the average salary paid in the South African community, social and personal
service industry was 10.179 Rand, excluding bonuses and overtime (Statistics South Africa,
2007: 20).

4.2.2.2 Staff Relations with Beneficiaries

Generally, the relationships between the TLF staff and the organization's beneficiaries are very close, friendly and personal rather than "professional". The
employees hold a very respectful view of the beneficiaries and strongly believe
in their capacities and assets. In many situations the staff does not only give but
also asks the beneficiaries for advice and help (INT: 4, 2, 5; O: 27.08.; 05.09.).
The TLF philosophy aims to create a feeling of equal partnership among staff
and beneficiaries and strongly discourages situations in which the staff has the
power and believes to be superior whereas the beneficiaries feel inferior and dependent. This philosophy is communicated to the staff, for example during the
devotions, by referring to the Christian principle that everyone is equal and
should be humble (before God) (O: 07.07.; see also TLF Values). According to
the TLF policy, staff members should therefore also commit themselves to a
simple life style (Blue File, Policy 5.3.1) in order to minimize the (economic)
differences between them and the beneficiaries (II: 20.07.; O: 08.09.).

TLF tries to further the aim of building and strengthening the bond between staff and beneficiaries by organizing common (recreational) events such
as the monthly celebration (II: 17.07.; O: 26.07.), a trip to the Gauteng Carnival
(O: 08.09.)[54] or the Spring Breakfast (O: 15.09.)[55]. On a day to day basis, the
celebration of beneficiaries' birthdays (O: 17.07.; 01.08.; II: 20.07.) or the hold-
ing of devotions (II: 11.07.; O: 05.09.) serves to create common, positive experiences.

As many of the staff come from difficult social backgrounds themselves
or have been TLF beneficiaries before becoming employees, they can really understand and relate to the problems of their beneficiaries. One interviewee explained the benefits of the TLF approach with regard to the relations between
staff and beneficiaries as following:

"[T]he (...) good thing about PCM is it takes the very same people that it serves and brings
them on board, you sit on the same table with those that you are serving now..., you no longer
call them beneficiaries but co-workers, for me that is a plus for an organization, one time they
were in the Potter's House and the next moment they become part of the team" (INT: 4)

The beneficiaries also describe their relationship with the staff as positive. They
feel that their problems and needs are well understood and taken care of, and
that the staff motivates and encourages them (INT: PH, LH1, LH3). Some ad-
mire the staff for their patience and admit that dealing with the beneficiaries and
their troubles is often very difficult, as the following quotation reveals:

"[T]hey are so kind and warm, they know how to handle problems, but sometimes we over-
power them because of our backgrounds from our bad family, they cannot change us, if you

---

[54] On this occasion a group of TLF staff and beneficiaries traveled to Johannesburg to participate in the Parade and the festivities in the context of the Gauteng Carnival which is a provi-
sional festival.
[55] On this day, all female staff and beneficiaries were invited to a Hotel in Pretoria to "celebrate their femininity". The women were served a lunch buffet and enjoyed a program designed to entertain but also empower, motivate and inform the women.

come from a rude home, it will be difficult for you to change being rude, they try by all means to change us…" (INT: PH)

But the beneficiaries also express criticism and accuse the staff of favoritism, stigmatization and gossiping (INT: PH, LH2). Some also feel misunderstood and do not trust the staff with their problems (INT: LH2, LH3). Despite all positive aspects, the relationships between staff and beneficiaries are also marked by (regular) mutual disappointments which jeopardize the relationship – for example, when a beneficiary falls back into bad habits (II/O: 23.07.; 13.08.; 27.08.) or when a staff member does not keep a promise (II/O: 17.07.; 13.09.).

The relationship between staff and beneficiaries plays a crucial role in an organizations approach to participation and empowerment. To further investigate this link, the concept of development brokers has been introduced and will be applied to the case of TLF in section 4.4.2.

4.2.2.3 Conflicts

When analyzing the conflicts concerning TLF, one can make a number of distinctions. On a very general level one can distinguish between *external* and *internal* conflicts. The most frequent and severe **external conflicts** occur between TLF and the City Council and usually center on issues of access, justice, power and exclusion (INT: 2, 3).

Conflicts within TLF happen between different groups and individuals, and result from various causes. The inner-organizational diversity is taken to be one reason for the existence of conflicts within TLF, which staff and management openly acknowledged. They generally regard conflicts as a natural and inherent part of community, which can even have a positive function when "well-managed" and solved (II/O: 05.07.; 13.07.). However, lately there has been a rise in the number of conflicts within TLF, which many attribute to the expansion of the organization and the growth of the workforce, and which they observe with worry (INT: 2, 3, 7). As a general rule, conflicts within TLF are dealt with according to the Disciplinary Code as expounded in the Blue File (INT: 2).

As mentioned in the definition of organizational culture (section 3.1.4), conflicts may be one indicator for the existence of subcultures within an organization. Furthermore, they reveal that the dominant organizational culture is by no means uncontested and universally accepted. In the following I will present some cases of conflicts which stand exemplary for deeper lines of contestation within TLF, and/ or provide examples for staff behavior that deviates from the official TLF ideology.

The most obvious deviation from the dominant organizational culture revealed itself in conflicts in which one side committed a serious violation of the TLF values. In two especially extreme cases, the "victims" (in one case a beneficiary, in the other case a staff member) were discriminated and stigmatized by individual TLF staff members on the grounds of their social problem (which was in both cases related to an HIV-infection). The "offenders" even tried to deny them their rightful access to help and resources (O: 19.07., II: 13.08.). This behavior presents a fundamental contradiction to the values of TLF which propagate community, compassion, justice and solidarity.

The most frequent conflicts, which were less severe but also difficult to solve, concerned work-related disputes, for example about how to operate a program, or when individual employees were accused of not doing their job properly. In most cases, these conflicts evolved from a different understanding of and/ or commitment to the TLF mission (O: 16.07.; 23.07.; 07.08.; 20.08.; 25.08.; II: 19.09.).

Conflicts between staff and management, which are frequently analyzed in organizational studies, also occurred within TLF, although not on a regular basis. One good example of such a conflict can be seen in the way the Feast of the Clowns 2007 was operated. Although the budget of the Feast was balanced for the first time due to the financial support from the city council, all events, workshops and activities were more expensive than in the previous years, especially for the staff who previously did not have to pay for most of the events at all. While the staff argued that they were expected to participate in the Feast activities and should therefore not be charged, the TLF management felt that the staff profited from the Feast and should therefore be willing to make a contribution and not take everything for granted (INT: 5, 7; O: 20.08.; 25.08.; 31.08.). Other, more latent conflicts between management and staff concerned the extent to which staff should have to commit themselves to the TLF cause and agree to make personal sacrifices in their private life (INT: 2, 5; O: 14.09.; II: 27.08.).

A very interesting conflict, especially in the context of development cooperation, occurred between the permanent staff and the international volunteers which often arose from intercultural misunderstandings, especially concerning different opinions of how the work should be efficiently managed. The German volunteers often felt frustrated as they perceived their working environment as "chaos", especially with regard to punctuality and communication issues, and believed that their efforts were not recognized and appreciated enough. The staff, on the other hand, sometimes felt irritated by volunteer's behavior and "lifestyle", concerning for example alcohol consumption, and "loose" (premarital) sexual relationships, which conflicted with the TLF values (INT: 6, 7; O: 04.07.; 21.08.; 07.09.; 08.09.; 19.09.).

Besides these obvious conflicts, there were also a number of latent tensions which unfolded at all levels of the organization, the most serious relating to racial issues and discrimination (II: 20.07.; O: 07.07.; 13.07.; 01.08.; 17.08.; 14.09.) Overall, it seems that in the past TLF managed its internal conflicts very effectively – through discussions, personal talks and, in extreme cases, through disciplinary measures. It remains to be seen, however, whether the recent increase in conflicts can be dealt with so that they do not negatively affect the work of TLF.

4.2.3 Material Aspects

Of the different materials elements of TLF's organizational culture (e.g. clothing, artifacts, fixtures) , I have chosen to focus on the architecture of the TLF "headquarters" as it reflects very visibly the egalitarian set up of the organization and the deliberate intent to not discriminate between management, staff and beneficiaries. The headquarters comprises the offices of the TLF management and administrative staff, a small meeting hall in which the weekly devotions are held, as well as the Potter's House. Furthermore, it includes the main office of Yeast City Housing (social housing company affiliated with TLF) and one of its residential facilities.

The Potter's House was intentionally built next to the TLF offices (II: 05.07.) and usually the doors between the two units are open so that many interactions take place between the TLF staff and the women staying in Potter's House. Many events in which both staff and beneficiaries participate (such as the monthly celebrations) are hosted in the headquarters. The architecture of the TLF headquarters presents a good indicator of the low hierarchies within the organization and the close relations between beneficiaries and staff.

4.3 Operational Approach

In the preceding sections, I have briefly depicted major elements of TLF's organizational culture. I will now outline TLF's working approach, especially with regard to participation and empowerment. In section 4.4, I will then systematically analyze how TLF's organizational culture affects its approach to participation and empowerment.

TLF's approach can be described as humanistic, holistic and inductive. Much effort is put into the identification and understanding of a problem, in which TLF relies to a large extent on the beneficiaries and involves other relevant stakeholders before suggesting solutions and initiating projects. The approach can be denoted holistic as TLF not only focuses on its immediate beneficiaries, but also provides support to their families. TLF acknowledges that an individual will unlikely profit from an intervention if he/ she stays in an unsupportive social environment. Therefore, employees of the shelters carry out visits to a beneficiary's home before and after taking him/ her into the program and try to address the problems found there (O: 24.07.; 26.07.). Another good example of the holistic approach can be found in Salvakop, where the Inkululeko kindergarten organizes workshops and events for the parents of the children attending, and tries to educate them on parenting issues (INT: 6).

TLF distances itself from conventional development or service organizations as described by McKnight[56] (1995) which pay "experts" to treat "people with deficiencies". As one informant states:

"[T]he negative thing about development I've seen in social work are that projects are not sustainable over long term, they usually had a developer, someone who knew everything, how it should look like, development should rather be a slow process where people develop themselves and get support from a person like a developer, who than just helps them to talk about what the issues are and where they want to go" (INT: 2)

---

[56] McKnight's article „Why servanthood is bad" was explicitly referred to by one informant. She explained that TLF uses it in trainings to remind TLF staff that servanthood can also be negative and patronizing when carried out with the wrong approach and for the wrong reasons (INT: 2).

The same interviewee describes the TLF approach as following:

"I think it's humility, and the breaking down of professionalism, in a sense of being professional but not being experts, not being helpers, but walking alongside people, (...) I mean when I look at other organizations there is a lot of 'come in to my office', there's counseling, it's very formal, there is a lot of helping happening, and experts telling people what to do, so I think in all the ministries with the homeless and everywhere we try to be more organizers, helping people to organize their lives, not even helping people, but facilitating space where people can help themselves" (INT: 2)

In order to identify communities and individuals that are in search of support, TLF has set up different outreaches. The outreach workers go out to places which are frequented by groups of people who live on the margins of society, face severe social problems and have often fallen through other support systems (which in South Africa are still based mainly on family ties). They pay visits to prostitutes working on the streets and in budget hotels (O: 11.07.; 21.08; 11.09.), to women and girls in prison (O: 29.08.; 19.09.), and to the mentally ill in West-koppies (a psychiatric sanatorium, O: 19.09.). They reach out to homeless people in Pretoria Central and in Marabastad, one of the poorest and most precarious areas of Pretoria, known for its thriving drug market, crime, violence and destitution (O: 05.07; 12.07.; 05.09.). And they enter "bad buildings" to search for victims of trafficking, abuse and forced (underage) prostitution, who are often detained there by there oppressors (INT: 2; II: 06.07.). TLF also maintains an outreach to economically and socially marginalized communities in the greater metropolitan area, for example in the former township of Cullinan (O: 03.08.; II: 30.07.; 06.09.)

The concept of the TLF outreach in some ways resembles the concept of participant observation applied in ethnography. It aims to gradually develop personal and trustful relationships with the beneficiaries, listen to what they identify as their problems and needs, and only then start to contrive plans for an intervention. On a regular (in most cases weekly) basis, the outreach workers spend some time with their target groups, listen to their stories, give them emotional and spiritual support, inform them about job and training opportunities or invite them to TLF events. This approach enables the TLF staff to remain in close contact with the beneficiaries, learn about how their problems and needs change, and keep updated on local developments (INT: 3, 4, 5).

The concept of having personal and close relationships with the beneficiaries does not only apply to the outreach work, but even more in the residential programs such as Lerato House. One German informant who has been working for TLF for seven years asserts:

„To study social work in Germany meant to learn about the importance of keeping a 'professional distance' in the first semester. The approach here is to deliberately say 'it is not like that', but to allow people to come close, I find that this is a more honest way to treat people, which makes it easier to recognize them and take them seriously, and therefore it also reveals their strengths and not only their deficits, I consider that really important, and those are the two reasons that keep me here, although often they are also the reasons which frustrate me the most" (INT: 7)[57].

The negative consequences are twofold: first, getting involved with the beneficiaries (and their problems) on a very personal level can be very (emotionally)
tiring and distressing (INT: 3, 5, 7). Secondly, having friendly rather than professional relationships makes it harder for staff to enforce rules and discipline
and to dismiss beneficiaries who have repeatedly violated regulations (O: 30.07.;
06.08.; 17.08.).

Besides the direct assistance of individuals and communities, TLF also
tries to facilitate farer reaching processes of Community Development and Citizenship Participation (see section 3.2.3). TLF has initiated and/ or been involved
in several forums and community associations, which are run by citizens and
present a channel for them to get involved in local politics. However, these forums have not always been successful, as they are strongly dependent on committed individuals. In many cases, decisions and suggestions which seem very
constructive and commendable are not being followed up properly and thus fail
to have an impact (INT: 2, 4, 6; O: 01.08.; 08.08.).

TLF strives to holistically address issues and problems which concern the
wider society. The Open Day Talk, an event organized by TLF during the (national) 16 days of activism campaign 2006, constitutes a good example. In order
to discuss how to reduce the extremely high prevalence of violence against and
abuse of women in the South African society, TLF invited not only women, but
also men (TLF Newsletter). An informant explains the idea behind the event:
"[L]ast year we realized that we are not doing much, we are working hard but we are not doing much, because we are concentrating only on women, everything is women women
women; women are being abused, women must do 1 2 3, you do this you won't be abused,
you keep on empowering our women but if you don't empower men it won't help anything,
still the abuse is going to happen, still men do not understand if they are doing anything
wrong, so we realized that and we also want to change it, last year during our Open Day Talk
we invited men, we asked the boys if they have been abused, how do they feel, and then we
asked men who never abuse their wives, what tactics that they use that they can tell other
men, we also have some men who in the beginning have been abusive and now they are fine,
how did they change it and what are they using, so we discussed around those lines" (INT: 5).

4.3.1 Participation
Within TLF participation seems to be an attitude rather than a tool or technical
method. In contrast to development organizations whose commitment to participation is largely rhetorical (see section 3.2.4), one can state that for TLF quite

---

[57] German original (the interview was conducted in German): „...in Deutschland Sozialpäda-
gogik, Sozialarbeit zu studieren hieß halt im ersten Semester zu hören, wie wichtig professio-
nelle Distanz ist, und das hier eben bewusst zu sagen „das ist nicht so", sondern Leute einfach
wirklich näher an sich ran zu lassen, ist ein ehrlicherer Umgang mit Leuten, finde ich, der die
Leute eher wahrnimmt und ernst nimmt, und damit eben auch auf die Stärken des anderen
gucken, und nicht nur die Defizite, das finde ich total wichtig, dass sind die beiden Gründe,
die mich hier halten, auch wenn es häufig die Gründe sind, die mich am meisten frustrie-
ren..." (INT: 7).

the opposite is the case: the approach of the organization (as outlined above) seems in fact very participatory although this is not officially explicated. In TLF documents, for example, one does not find explicit references to participation.

One can best analyze if and how TLF practices participation by looking at the relationships between staff and beneficiaries more closely, and by investigating how TLF staff members delineate participation. For the interviewees, who I asked for a definition, participation (ideally) meant that staff and beneficiaries come together on the same level and that everyone is involved in the decision-making process and the realization of plans and projects. According to them, participation also entails creating space for (marginalized) people to express themselves (INT: 3, 4, 5, 6). One informant commented on the difficulties of an organization being truly participatory, and explained how TLF tries to apply a practicable approach to participation:

"[T]hat is something you have to evaluate all the time - how do you let people participate? Giving them complete access to information, and being completely open, not keeping information secret, so complete participation would be a real open process, real democratic in terms of how decisions are made, although that becomes very difficult (...) so there is a measure of democracy and authority, and that could be a positive authority in a certain sense, there's a circle of people doing things together but that there is also someone in the middle, who sometimes says 'this way', who sees the map, who has to see the whole and know where to go just at that moment" (INT: 2)

Within the TLF programs, participation is of relevance with regard to two aspects of the day-to-day work: first, it relates to the joint identification of problems, needs and assets of the beneficiaries as well the reflection about possible solutions. As outlined above, this is mainly realized through the outreach program. Home visits constitute another method to uncover needs and constraints of a beneficiary and his/ her family (O/ II: 24.07.; 26.07.).

Secondly, participation plays a role in relation to the ongoing programs and decisions which have to be taken on a daily basis. Here, different types of meetings serve to facilitate participation. In Potter's House and Lerato House, the women and girls respectively, meet weekly with the staff (INT: 3, 5). In Lerato House, attendance is compulsory. The meetings are chaired by a staff member and minuted by one of the girls. At the beginning, everyone has the chance to put up agenda points, which are then discussed in the course of the meeting. While some girls really use the meetings to voice ideas or criticize developments in Lerato House, others, who are not so outspoken, usually keep quite (O: 16.07.; 23.07.; 30.07.; 03.09.; 10.09.; 17.09.). In an interview, one of the girls explained:

"[T]he thing is, most of the girls in the house are very scared of each other, especially the smaller ones they don't like to talk in the house meeting, cause why? They are scared of us, the older ones (...), we used to bully them, not all of us, but some of us they would shout at them (...) I think it is better for them [the younger girls] to go to the social worker or the councilor to talk about it [their concern], maybe the social worker can organize something with the staff or maybe talk to them, then they can raise it in their meetings, or in our meetings, but they mustn't be specific about who said that" (INT: LH2).

This quotation reveals that the extent to which beneficiaries (can) participate is very much dependent on the situational context and the capacity of individual staff to pay attention and involve those who might otherwise be left out. At the Inkululeko day care center, parent-teacher meetings take place once a term, where parents have the chance to express concerns or make suggestions about the program. Parents can also write propositions and put them in the "suggestion box", which is accessible all year round. However, many parents do not attend and make use of the opportunity to participate, one possible reason being their low educational background (INT: 6). As specified in section 3.2.4, the lack of will to participate presents a common obstacle to achieve participatory development, which also applies to some beneficiaries of TLF (O: 23.07.; 23.08.; 27.08.).

Within TLF, neither the outreach and the family visits nor the meetings explicitly intend to implement participation in the technical sense, but are expressions of a more general belief in the importance of long-term, close and egalitarian relationships and regular exchanges between staff and beneficiaries (II: 17.07.; 21.08.; 11.09.). During my fieldwork, I got the impression that the methods usually associated with the concept of participation such as PRA, RRA or ZOPP (see section 3.2.3) were largely unknown to the majority of staff (O: 20.08.). Although the employees in the various projects were aware that programs could not be planned for others but had to be developed together with the beneficiaries (O: 10.09.), they did not have a comprehensive set of participatory tools which to apply. Surveys and questionnaires constituted the only systematic methods which were occasionally utilized to intentionally reveal the opinion of beneficiaries. As one informant specified:

"[W]e once had a very strategic and intentional survey, which was mainly done in Plantana[58], that was one thing since I started working here that I saw we intentionally did, but in terms of really saying now we are going out to find out what are the needs of this community, no, (…) we don't really…" (INT: 3).

Another informant, who is working for a different project maintained:

"[I]n our planning we involve the beneficiaries, they do the evaluation of the projects, we give them some kind of questionnaire which they then answer, they participate, they have a say, we do consultations with the beneficiaries in terms of programs." but then added: "I would love to (…) maybe work out a program that is systematic, where every three or four months the beneficiaries can do an evaluation, maybe we need to come to that point, we are not yet there" (INT: 4).

The level and extent of staff participation provides another good indicator to assess how participatory an organization operates. Due to the relatively egalitarian structures within the projects and the organization as a whole, decisions are rarely taken in a top-down fashion, but usually evolve from common debates

---

[58] Plantana is a building next to Lerato House, mainly inhabited by people with a low income and low social status. As a result of the survey TLF set up a crèche where parents, staying at Plantana, can bring their children when they are looking for employment as this was identified as one the biggest needs of the people.

among staff and management. On the (lowest) project level, staff meetings are held on a weekly basis and serve to discuss concerns and suggestions relating to the project but also to TLF as a whole. In general, all staff members *can* not only freely express their opinion on all the matters discussed but are strongly encouraged to do so (O: 09.07.; 16.07.; 06.08.; 03.09.). The same applies to the devotions, which also provide a platform for staff to come together and confer about organizational issues.

When talking about staff participation within TLF, the interviewees often referred to the *planning cycle*. In September, all staff members of each ministry participate in an internal evaluation of their program and discuss plans for the next year. They present their ideas to the whole of TLF at the end-of-the-year-retreat in November. From November until January, a concrete business-plan (including the annual budget) for each program is set up by the management and coordinators. This is then again presented to the whole staff that can give inputs, make comments and ask questions on what has been worked out. Finally, the business-plans are taken to the board, which has to approve them for the new financial year which starts in April. During the mid-year-retreat in July, a (participatory) intermediary evaluation of the programs takes place (INT: 2, 3, 4, 6).

TLF has mechanisms which ensure that even the initiation of big, new programs is done in a participatory manner. One informant explained how these can come into being:

"I think new ideas can come from anyone, (…) they [the staff in the projects] know the issues so they come back to the management, they would first discuss it in their staff meetings and say we should do this or we should do that (…) whatever ideas they think is great for developing their programs, their coordinator would bring it to the management, management would discuss if that is viable, they wouldn't argue in terms of program issues, but they would argue in terms of money, space, time frame, capacity of staff, so they would ask the questions, then (…) we would in the management say 'ok, let's start a committee', so the committee comes from interested people and people who have skills to do this kind of thing, to initiate a program, so it could be anyone in the organization, it don't need to be the senior people, anyone in the organization, (…) so if there is a committee then there eventually needs to be a proposal and then the proposal needs to go to the board of TLF who has to make the final decision, so we need to have a budget and where we want to do this and staff, everything has to be really detailed, that would be for the start of a big new program; smaller things, the ministries can do their own thing" (INT: 2).

One downside of these participatory processes - concerning both, staff and beneficiary participation - is that they take a lot of time and energy (INT: 2, 3; II: 10.07.; 17.07.). Another problem relates to the realization of the suggestions discussed in the meetings. It is often frustrating to see that so many good ideas are not being followed up or are carried out lackadaisically, and are thus discarded (O: 23.07.; 26.07.; 01.08.; 06.08.; 08.08.; 10.09.; 14.09.). Furthermore, TLF - in many cases - does not possess the resources which would be necessary to implement the ideas (INT: PH; O/ II: 03.09.; 11.09.).

In sum, one can deduce that TLF follows an "inherent" rather than a systematic approach to beneficiary participation in the narrow sense – meaning the application of specific tools and methods to facilitate identifying the needs and interests of the beneficiaries. The participation of staff is encouraged and promoted rather systematically although, in the literature on participatory development, this does not represent a common indicator of an organization's commitment to participation (see section 3.2).

On a more general level, the TLF approach corresponds to (newer) participatory concepts such as community and institutional development, collective empowerment and citizenship participation (see table 1, p. 28). As stated in the TLF information flyer

"[t]he Tshwane Leadership Foundation was created to strengthen the unfolding church-based social movement, and to provide more strategic and proactive leadership in the City of Tshwane and beyond regarding urban ministry and urban community development".

The initiators of TLF and those, who are now in the management, have a very comprehensive understanding of the ongoing discourses on development, civil society and social movements. They try very systematically to incorporate their expert knowledge into the conception of the TLF programs (INT: 2; O: 06.07.; 07.07.; Krige, 2007: 79f.). Yet, the fact that most of the staff does not have an academic education sometimes impedes their efforts, as the staff members do not always understand the ideas behind the programs and thus have difficulties in implementing them. However, as demonstrated above, the in some aspects "disorderly development dynamic" (Krige, 2007: 136) which results from this, seems a lot more participatory and democratic than the "technical" approaches followed by many development organizations. In his final analysis of the organization, Krige (ibid: 134f.) concludes that

"TLF is not only (…) influencing policy and practices towards strengthening community-based structures and operations, but there is also a drive towards becoming a social or people's movement (…) which is not driven by money, budgets, and institutional performance but by vision, values, innovative ideas, social energy, reinforcing synergy and dynamic networks. Social movements must be seen as key to transformational change."

TLF's commitment to concepts such as community development and citizenship participation is also revealed in the organization's approach to empowerment.

4.3.2 Empowerment
TLF's approach to empowerment is more strategic and intentional than the organization's approach to participation. Empowerment is explicitly mentioned as a key objective of TLF's work in official documents and on the TLF website. TLF adheres to a holistic empowerment approach and aims to empower its beneficiaries economically, educationally, socially and spiritually.

Vocational trainings and job referrals are the most important instruments for **economic empowerment**. Vocational trainings such as courses for cooking, sowing, business and computer skills are often organized internally, through the Institute of Urban Ministry which is part of TLF (see graphic 3, p. 48) or by one of the projects (Akanani, for example, organizes computer and business skills courses on a regular basis). In other cases, trainings are organized in cooperation with other institutions, for example with other shelters or with the governmental

Department of Social Development (INT: 4; O/ II: 11.07.; 01.08.; 14.08.). Referring beneficiaries into jobs presents a bigger challenge for TLF as the organization is thereby always dependent on external contacts (II: 03.09.; 11.09.). Therefore, the support given to the beneficiaries is mainly indirect: TLF offers assistance in searching for employment offers on the job market as well as in writing CVs and applications. Many beneficiaries work for TLF as cleaning or kitchen staff before they enter the external job market. Some also stay in the organization and, depending on their qualifications, end up in all sorts of positions. The intentional aiming for beneficiaries to become staff presents a distinctive empowerment approach of TLF.

TLF also provides different forms of **educational empowerment**. It pays the school fees for the girls in Lerato House and for the children of the women in Potters House who would otherwise probably not receive schooling. The younger children obtain an early childhood education either from one of the two TLF crèches or by attending the Inkululeko kindergarten. Furthermore, beneficiaries are given the opportunity to participate in workshops or conferences where they can acquire life skills (on a very general level) or more specific information, for example on topics like HIV/ Aids or gender (INT: 3, 5; O/ II: 02.08.; 13.08.; 03.09.).

TLF encourages beneficiaries to participate in devotions and self-help groups which are intended to **empower** them **spiritually**. In these group-sessions, the beneficiaries learn to talk about their problems and are taught that they can find redemption and support in God. As practically none of the TLF staff members are trained as therapists, spiritual (religious) affirmation often seems to be the only way to give comfort and help a beneficiary to deal with experienced traumas (O/ II: 30.07.; 29.08.; 11.09.; 17.09.). Devotions are a central part of all the social programs at TLF, and beneficiaries are expected to attend (here the missionary element in the work of TLF becomes most clearly visible).

Social empowerment is an umbrella term for various events and activities organized by TLF which aim to (re)integrate people into society who live on the margins, and help them develop a positive attitude towards life. Happenings, such as the Feast of the Clowns or the Spring Breakfast, give these people the possibility to participate in a form of social and cultural life from which many of them would normally be excluded. The newly set-up School of Creative Arts offers free dance, poetry, theatre and music classes especially for young people. One aim is to get teenagers and adolescents off the streets and give them a chance to develop their talents (INT: 4; II: 05.07.; O: 24.07.).

By following this holistic empowerment approach, TLF aims to gradually prepare the beneficiaries for a future in which they will not receive institutional support. Thereby, TLF tries to build on the assets the beneficiaries bring with them. One informant explains:

"Well, empowerment (...) is not to actually bring something new, new power if I may put it like that, but it is to stimulate the power that lies within each and every individual, because I believe that each and every individual has a potential, a skill and a gift, god-given talent, so empowerment is just stimulating, inspiring, motivating a person to take charge of the capabilities that lie dormant, but that they are not aware of in their own personal lives" (INT: 6).

One reason for which TLF propagates this idea of asset-based empowerment is that the organizations wants to prevent creating relationships of dependency, which often result from conventional development and social work efforts (INT: 2) as explained by one interviewee:

"I think the women [in Potter's House] really have to do everything for themselves, what we do is just to direct them, when they come at the in-take we tell them everything that is happening, and then the woman will choose what she wants to do, we ask them what have you done before, from there we will discuss and see what she can go on doing, we don't want to do things for women cause it is making them more dependent, but we make them see that they can do it, cause that is what they are missing out there, so then they are here, we make them realize that 'oh, I can do it', so we help them to do it, if it is that they are stuck and it is difficult, then we direct them" (INT: 5).

Evidently, there are limits to empowerment. If beneficiaries are not willing to make an effort and take responsibility for their lives, even the most holistic and asset-based empowerment approach will eventually fail (INT: 3, 5). However, due to the often severe problems the beneficiaries face when they come to TLF, many are lethargic and completely discouraged and thus need time to recover themselves. TLF has come to understand that

"there is a style that really does not work (...) and that is to tell someone 'listen, pull up your socks, you can do it, come on, you're a mature adult person, come on, you can do it, I wanna see results next week', that kind of motivation does not work, I've seen it from experience, it is really like a slap in the face for people, because the issues are so complex, and it is again a holistic thing, if they are not emotionally stable, feel safe here, that is the other thing, if you have people in your programs and they are dependent on you, you should really make them feel safe, you cannot say to them 'next month you're out, goodbye, and if you don't find a job it is your problem and you need to decide where to go', that anxiousness and anxiety and stress is just too much, it paralyses them" (INT: 2).

All the beneficiaries I spoke to in the course of my fieldwork, especially those in the (temporary) residential facilities, very much appreciated the empowerment approach of TLF. They were grateful for the programs they were offered and affirmed that they had profited a lot from their "encounter" with TLF (INT PH, LH1, LH2, LH3). The following two quotations are illuminating:

"[T]hey [TLF] empower people, they really empower the victims, if you know what you want from life when you get out of this place you know what life is all about, you do appreciate that your problem is much better than other people's problems, that's what I like about Potter's House" (INT: PH).

"[I]t [empowerment] makes me wake up from sleeping, it makes me be, believe in myself, say that I also have the power because of the power they give me from Lerato House, the courage, you can name it all, all those words I can't think of maybe" (INT: LH3)

Although it is not always evident, TLF does make an impact on the lives of the beneficiaries. By far not all manage to change their lives; some go back to life on the streets, to drugs or to prostitution. But most of the beneficiaries experience positive moments during their encounter with TLF which make a difference for them - if only for a short while (INT 3, 4, 6; O: 22.08.; 24.08.; 25.08.; 31.08.; 05.09.; 08.09.; II: 11.09.). Realistically, there is only so much TLF can achieve for the individual due to the huge structural constraints like poverty, un-employment or abuse faced by most beneficiaries *and* due to a lack of resources as well as a shortage of qualified social workers and therapists within TLF.

Besides the empowerment of the individual, TLF also aspires to initiate community empowerment on a broader scale. The annual organization of an "environment day" in Salvokop presents a good example. There, the whole community is encouraged to participate in a clean-up campaign and learns to take ownership of their surroundings. The event is also supported by the local government (INT: 6; O/ II: 06.07.). Furthermore, TLF assists the residents of Salvakop in their negotiations with the government on housing issues. Due to the newly build Freedom Park Monument (which is expected to become a great tourist attraction after its opening in 2009), the city council wants to remove the large number of squatters in the area without providing alternative living spaces for them. TLF not only helps the people to register for RDP housing[59], but also motivates them to get involved in the decision-making processes concerning the development of the area (INT: 6).

Empowerment efforts of TLF not only target beneficiaries, but are also aimed at staff. Every permanent staff member is strongly encouraged to further his/ her skills and qualifications (TLF Policy 14, see Blue File). There are compulsory as well as optional courses offered, for example, by the Institute of Urban Ministry, and many (shorter) one- or two-day workshops. TLF aspires to develop new leaders, not only for the organization but also for the wider community. Therefore, the organization also supports the tertiary education of staff. At the time of my research several employees, in addition to their day-to-day work, were doing courses at UNISA[60] in order to obtain a degree (II/ O: 11.07.; 13.07.; 16.07.; 18.07.).

On the negative side, this puts a lot of pressure on those employees who are both working and studying, and sometimes leads to situations in which they either have to neglect their studies or their job. Some staff members, especially those in lower positions and those who come from very low educational backgrounds, do not make use of the training opportunities given to them or do not take them seriously enough (INT: 5; O/ II: 07.07.; 09.07.; 28.08.; 14.09.).

In sum, TLF follows a comprehensive approach to empowerment which not only targets the individual beneficiaries, but aims to build and strengthen civil-society activism and initiate structural change and transformation on a broader scale.

---

[59] The Reconstruction and Development Programme (RDP) is an integrated socio-economic policy framework adopted by the South African Government after the end of the apartheid. Among several other things, it aims for the building of new, low-cost houses for economically marginalized groups of the population as specified in the "New Housing Policy and Strategy for South Africa", see www.info.gov.za/whitepapers/1994/housing.htm.

[60] The University of South Africa is a one of the largest distance education institutions in the world.

4.4 The Influence of Organizational Culture on Participation and Empowerment in the Case of TLF

4.4.1 Professionalization and Bureaucratization

In section 3.3.1, the following hypothesis was established on the effect of professionalization and bureaucratization on an organization's ability to initiate participatory and empowering development:

The more professional and bureaucratic an organization is or becomes, the more difficulties it will have in establishing/ maintaining close relationships to its beneficiaries and grassroots supporters and in rendering the development process participatory and empowering.

In the subsequent paragraphs, I will analyze to what extent this hypothesis seems compelling when applied to the case of TLF. First, I will examine the level of professionalism and bureaucratization TLF has reached, and secondly, I will scrutinize how this affects the organization's approach to participation and empowerment.

As identified in section 3.3.1, there are many indicators which suggest that an organization has entered a phase of professionalization and bureaucratization: an increase in staff, offices and budget; a standardization of procedures; and a change in the recruitment principles. The latter entails that educational qualifications become more important than ideological commitment and that formerly voluntary positions are filled with permanent staff.

According to these indicators, one can say that TLF is in a process of professionalization and bureaucratization. Between 1993 and 2007 the number of staff members has, on average, grown 17.5% annually. Within the last five years the TLF budget has more than doubled and increased from 1.7 million Rand in 2001/2 to 4.2 million Rand in 2006/7. Since its beginnings in 1993, TLF has gradually extended its range of programs, broadened its partnerships and steadily gained influence in the social work and development sector of Tshwane (Krige, 2007: 76ff.; INT: 4, 6).

There are some indications for an incipient standardization and formalization of procedures and staff recruitment principles within TLF. Policy as well as grievance procedures have been established. At the time of my research, the disciplinary guidelines were being revisited, including the development of new sanction and enforcement mechanisms. These became necessary in order to be able to control the growing number of staff members, and as the staff's compliance with the rules could no longer be settled informally (INT: 2; II: 03.09.; 10.09.). Furthermore, new (permanent) staff has been employed and is still sought in the administration sector – e.g. for IT, finance and logistics (INT: 7; II: 06.07.) - taking over tasks which were formerly carried out by volunteers. Job descriptions of most staff and business plans have been refined and serve as tools to evaluate an employee's work rather than just continuing to be vague and discarding documents as before. During my stay, management started to scrutinize the contracts of all staff as it had turned out that some employees had been working without contracts and had thus been able to resign without giving prior notice (O/ II: 16.07./ 03.09.). Other signs of an increasing bureaucratization within TLF include, for example, that the staff in the projects has to devote more and more time to writing reports and calculating statistics and spends a huge proportion of each working week in meetings (O: 09.07.; 30.07.; 20.08.; 27.08.).

The initiation of these developments is still fairly recent and very much contested and questioned among both staff and management. However, becoming more professional is essential for TLF in order to exert influence and have an impact on developments in Tshwane and to gain and increase access to funding.

As outlined in section 3.3.1 the adaptation to the institutional environment and structures, may be essential for an organization to be recognized by other organizations or the state. Thus, one can speak of an external pressure to institutionalize and professionalize which evidently affects TLF. This is especially evident with regard to the Department of Social Development. The department is, for example, attempting to bring the different shelters of Tshwane together under one superstructure. This entails that the individual shelters have to homogenize procedures, reports and statistics as dictated by the department. Furthermore, the department has installed a regular supervision for each shelter. As the local government is one of TLF's main funders, the organization has to adapt to the demands of the department, at least to some extent (O: 16.07.; 19.07; 27.07.; 27.08.).

Similar external pressures to professionalize and institutionalize are exerted by other funders – among them highly bureaucratic institutions such as the European Union or the International Labor Organization (INT: 2, 7). In order to live up to their standards, TLF needs to augment the quantity and quality of reports, presentations and statistics. Furthermore, public relations and donor management as well as marketing, advocacy and lobbying efforts require improvement. Currently, however, TLF lacks qualified staff which would be able to adapt to such standards. Many have little to no computer skills, speak a low level of English and are not trained in communications, lobbying or marketing (INT: 4, 5, 6, 7; O/ II: 31.07.; 28.08.). Therefore, reports and presentations given by staff sometimes do not match donor requirements; events organized by TLF often seem chaotic and could be more successful if the organizational and marketing capacities were improved. Professionalization could lead to more efficiency and less confusion, not only with regard to TLF's external affairs, but also internally, in the day-to-day work. At present, much time and effort is wasted as people do not keep appointments, pass on information or execute the tasks assigned to them (O: 06.07.; 25.07.; 31.07.; 02.08.; 27.08.).

On the negative side, professionalization leads (and already has led) to profound changes in the values of TLF and the relationships between staff, beneficiaries and management as described by one informant:

"In the first years, when I came for the first time in 1995/96, community - that was everybody, we weren't so many then, a few homeless and the women [in Potter's House] and the staff, I think we were seven [staff members] in total. Eating lunch and dinner together was normal and no big thing, but now, because of the size of the organization, it is difficult to organize something like that (…) It is crucial to create awareness of the importance of the exchange between staff and beneficiaries, it is one of the points we have to focus on more, because stuff like donor management, for which reports, statistics etc. become necessary, costs so much time that personal interactions are neglected. **Then, it happens much faster that one forgets to render the house meetings participatory, for example;** because of the workload one rather decides to say 'these are the problems we need to speak about with the women and girls'. To create an atmosphere where they feel that they are a part and can also exert influence is important, but difficult to maintain, I think..." (INT: 7; emphasis added)[61].

One finds that professionalization may correlate negatively with the level of participation as it does not always present the most efficient way of handling things (see also INT: 2). TLF's approach to participation centers on the idea of being an inclusive community. Professionalization, however, aims for the creation of competent institutions in which relationships which are primarily work-related. Success is measured by efficiency and incentives to work based on financial rewards rather than commitment to an ideal or a cause.

During the mid-year retreat, TLF's managing director reflected on the difficulties of becoming more professional while at the same time staying a community which is committed to specific values and a certain ideology. He advocated that TLF would have to find a middle way and try to "live the tension". Despite the inherent dangers, he maintained that professionalization was important as "funders don't give money to communities with nice visions but to transparent organizations" (O: 06.07.). Some employees, however, doubt that finding a middle way presented a viable solution. One informant alleged that

"PCM needs to decide if we want to be a charity or an institution, (...) because at the rate that we are losing people it is cause we want to be both, and we cannot maintain both especially when it comes to the business people, we fail to maintain those, but we need to be at peace if we say we want to be a charity, we need to then say this is who we are and this is who we want to be and be in peace with it, but if we say no no no, then we have to carry the consequences, meaning we have to raise our salaries, we have to have our structures very structured and very strict, not so loose as they are now" (INT: 3).

The same interviewee diagnosed finding qualified staff which is committed to the organization's ideals and willing to work for a low salary as one of the key challenges for TLF:

---

[61] German original: „... in den ersten Jahren, als ich 95-96 zum ersten Mal hier war, da war so Community, das waren wir alle, da waren es ja noch nicht so viele, ein paar Obdachlose und die Frauen und die MA, wir alle waren damals sieben glaube ich, und da war zusammen Mittag essen und Abendbrot essen ganz normal und kein Ding, und das mit der Größe der Organisation in der Form jetzt hin zu kriegen ist schwierig, (...) [dass] das Bewusstsein geschaffen wird zum Austausch zwischen MA und beneficiaries ist total wichtig und ist definitiv einer der Punkte, wo wir viel viel mehr, oder offensiver gucken müssen, weil es halt gerade auch durch so Klamotten wie Donor Management, weil da halt auch ständig irgendwelche Berichte, Statistiken (...) anstehen, und das einfach so viel Zeit wegnimmt, dass das Persönliche einfach ganz schnell in den Hintergrund treten kann und man deshalb viel leichter vergisst, die Hausmeeting wirklich participatory zu machen, zum Beispiel, sondern einfach durch die Workload sagt ‚das und das und das sind Probleme, da müssen wir mit den Frauen oder den Mädels drüber sprechen', aber dann eine Atmosphäre zu schaffen, wo sie dann das Gefühl haben, Teil sein zu können und shapen zu können ist wichtig aber schwierig aufrecht halten zu können, denke ich..." (INT: 7).

"I think at PCM they sometimes think that committed people win, they develop and make the organization successful, but sometimes committed people lack the skills, for me I think we need both – we need to be skillful and committed" (INT: 3).

Some TLF members voiced the concern that an increasing number of staff members, especially those who had been recently employed, were less committed to the values of TLF and less willing to make sacrifices for their work (INT: 2, 3, 4, 7; O: 06.07.; 01.08.). It appeared that these employees saw their work as a "normal profession" and not as a calling and a passion. They seemed unsatisfied with the working conditions, felt underpaid and passed all responsibilities to their superiors. Formerly, when the workforce was still smaller and TLF was less professional and institutionalized, everybody was happy just to be a part of the TLF community. Today, the community model of TLF, in which the relations between staff and beneficiaries are friendly rather than professional and both share a similar living situation (also financially), is no longer supported unconditionally by *all* staff members. This is also revealed in a high level of staff fluctuation, which presents a fundamental problem for TLF. During the period of my research, many employees, some in central positions, quit and left TLF. As finding replacements proved difficult, volunteers had to take over (some of) these positions (INT: 7; O/ II: 04.07.; 30.08.; 10.09.). Furthermore, the rising number of conflicts among staff, centering on issues of jealousy, racism or other forms of discrimination, indicates a weakening of the TLF community model (O: 13.07.; 06.08.).

All in all, TLF seems to be a case which supports the above stated hypothesis. Within the organization, there are obvious indicators of an insetting professionalization and increasing bureaucratization. These threaten the community model to which TLF adheres and on which its approach to participation and empowerment centers. The relationships between staff are becoming more conflictive as not everyone agrees on the strategies and principals adopted by TLF. In order to maintain discipline, hierarchies are becoming more important, and more often decisions are taken in a top-down manner – both, between management and staff as well as between staff and beneficiaries. In general, the relationships between staff and beneficiaries are still very close and intact although mutual exchanges and common activities have become less frequent due to the growth of the organization. As the work becomes more sophisticated and requires skilled professionals, it seems probable if not inevitable that fewer beneficiaries will become TLF employees and that the organization's unique concept of empowerment will eventually run out. TLF finds itself confronted with a dilemma: if the organization wants to gain influence and really make an impact it has to adapt to the dominant institutional system and "play by the rules" which means it has to professionalize and bureaucratize. This, however, means that TLF has to give up or neglect some of its original values and concepts, especially those which lie at the heart of a true participation and empowerment approach.

4.4.2 Development Brokers

Three hypotheses were drawn regarding the impact of development brokers on the successful realization of participation and empowerment (see section 3.3.2):

1. The more skillful the broker is in translating between the implementing organization and the stakeholders at the local level, the greater are the chances that a project represents a negotiated consensus rather than a top-down enforcement.
2. The more interrelations take place between developers and beneficiaries, the easier it becomes for the broker to facilitate participation.
3. The more compatible the culture(s) of the developers and the culture(s) of the beneficiaries are, the easier it becomes for the broker to facilitate participation.

In order to assess the relevance of these hypotheses regarding the case of TLF, it seems constructive to first examine the *levels* as well as the *processes* of brokerage within the organization.

One can analyze two main *levels* of brokerage within TLF: between external funders and TLF, and between TLF and its beneficiaries. As stated in section 3.3.2, relations of brokerage resemble to some extent patron-client relationships, which implies that power between the two sides is unequally distributed and one side is more dependent on the relationship than the other.

Evidently, the funders of TLF can exert some control on the organization's approach and programs, simply by denying to allocate the money requested from them. However, in comparison with other development funding organizations which send their own experts to advise the local organization and manage and coordinate the programs, their influence is fairly limited. The relationship of brokerage is reduced to negotiations about funds between the TLF management and the responsible personnel in the funding organization. In order to convince funders of the TLF approach, gain their trust, and make them understand the benefits of the organization's values and working procedures, the TLF managers attempt to make these relationships as personal as possible as the following quote reveals:

"The (...) thing is to make the relationship personal, that's something we learned over the years, (...) not like friendly, chatty, but in a sense getting to know the people behind the funds, (...) writing emails and talking about their children, (...) when people come to visit, you go out to eat together, (...) but not all donors are like that, some are much more formal and power orientated, so you struggle to break down that whole relationship, but we try" (INT: 2).

Getting involved with funders on a personal level can be described as a form of "upward participation" as it constitutes an attempt to "incorporate" the funders into the TLF community rather than just taking their money.

With regard to the second level of brokerage - between TLF and its beneficiaries - the TLF staff can be delineated as brokers. Their skills and efforts are crucial in ensuring that TLF can realize its objectives. They also have to make sure that the needs and demands of the beneficiaries are taken into account and their expectations are fulfilled. As already depicted, TLF does not want to be regarded as a conventional development agency which employs "experts telling other people what to do" but rather aspires for its employees to be "organizers, helping people to organize their lives, not even helping people, but facilitating space where people can help themselves" (INT: 2). Therefore, TLF emphasizes the similarities between staff and beneficiaries and stresses that these outweigh the (potential) differences. One informant described that in contrast to development operations where international development experts work together with local staff (she mentioned the programs of the GTZ as an example),

"TLF does not have these two sides. Instead, the people come from everywhere, many are local, from the community, and thus there are more common starting points, the similar background of the people facilitates working together and understanding each other, therefore the work relations are much more personal, and the cooperation and partnership work..." (INT: 1).[62]

In one of his sermons, the managing director stressed that everyone - no matter if rich or poor, vulnerable or powerful, deprived or privileged – may face difficulties at some point in life, and that the common experience of suffering and feeling broken is what connects people more than their material and outward differences (O: 07.07.). He added that rather than employing and creating development experts, TLF wants staff members to be leaders, who demonstrate servitude instead of control, brokenness instead of power, and hospitality instead of competitiveness (ibid). All the program coordinators I interviewed understood their role as being catalysts, facilitators and "brokers" between the project staff and the beneficiaries, and saw their main duty in supervising the staff to ensure that the beneficiaries received a good service (INT: 3, 4, 5, 6).

Regarding the levels of brokerage, analyzing the "classical dichotomy of development cooperation" between "internationals" and "locals" is of lesser importance concerning the case of TLF. Very few of the organization's employees come from overseas (although those who do generally occupy central positions). The majority of the international staff are volunteers, who have a limited influence on organizational issues. Nevertheless, the volunteers do in some cases expose attitudes and behaviors which resemble those of international development experts, and which mirror many of the problems occurring in conventional development cooperation, especially with regard to participation. Examples include insisting on western standards and working procedures, acting in a top-down manner or not accepting values and worldviews which differ from their own. Due to their often superior educational background (when compared with the majority of the staff), the volunteers often (and not always intentionally) take or are given the role of the advisor and organizer. Intercultural misunderstandings and different perceptions of what constitutes a successful and organized program, occasionally lead to conflicts among permanent staff and volunteers (INT: 7; O/ II: 04.07.; 14./15.07.; 01.08.; 31.07.; 20.08., 21.08., 25.08., 28.08.; 05.09.; 08.09.; 13.09.; 19.09.; see also Krige, 2007: 98f.).

---

[62] German original: „Bei TLF hingegen (...) gibt [es] also nicht so zwei Seiten, sondern es gibt Leute von überall her, viele sind local, aus der Community selbst, und dadurch gibt es viel mehr Ansatzpunkte, wo sich die Leute sowieso schon ähnlich sind, zusammen arbeiten, sich verstehen, und deshalb läuft die Arbeit viel persönlicher ab, die Zusammenarbeit funktioniert besser..." (INT: 1).

I will now turn to the *processes* of brokerage within TLF. These can be best exemplified by looking at the TLF planning cycle which has already been outlined in section 4.3.1. Hereby, multiple processes of brokerage become obvious and reveal that, in fact, there are more than just the two main levels of brokerage introduced above. The underlying idea of the planning cycle is that beneficiaries voice their ideas to the project staff, who passes them on to the coordinators. The coordinators ensure that the issues are taken up by the management which then refers them to the board. The board finally decides if and how to implement the suggested measures. (Where the different funders come into this cycle probably depends on the type of project and the sum which is required but as I did not gain a deeper insight into this question during my research I will refrain from speculating about it.) In the interviews, some informants mentioned projects which had been successfully planned and implemented according to the principles of the planning cycle (INT: 2, 3, 5). One can find several more examples of processes of brokerage in the day-to-day work, which will, however, not be listed here.

Finally, I will now evaluate the explanatory power of the hypotheses with regard to the case of TLF. Hereby, I will concentrate on the brokerage between TLF and its beneficiaries, because (as already specified) I did not have the opportunity to get a closer look at the relations between TLF and its funders.

The first hypothesis implies that successful brokerage depends heavily on the skills of the individual broker. This applies very much to the case of TLF – during my research I noticed several times how much the participation of beneficiaries and, more generally, the success of programs, differed depending on which staff members were involved. Most TLF employees made great efforts to ensure that the programs were participatory and that the opinion of the beneficiaries was not only noticed but also acted upon. Some, however, just tried to get their work done with the least possible effort, which also entailed that they made decisions for the beneficiaries in order to evade long discussions and possible alterations of the plans. (O/ II: 12.07.; 16.07.; 23.07.; 02.08.; 06.08.; 20.08.; 29.08.; 17.09.). In some cases, the implementation of ideas and plans also failed because the staff lacked the skills or (more often) the commitment to accomplish it (O: 26.07.; 23.07.; 14.09.). Therefore, one can conclude that not only the skillfulness but also the willingness and the commitment of the broker determine whether the opinions of the beneficiaries are passed on to higher levels in the organization and to what extent they are successfully implemented.

Hypotheses 2 and 3 suggest that the extent to which brokers successfully manage to translate and reconcile the demands of the different development stakeholders depends on how far the standpoints, ideas and interests of beneficiaries, staff and management (and also of the funders) are compatible. It also depends on the frequency (and intensity) of the interrelations which take place between them. As recurrently outlined, the close and personal relationships between staff and beneficiaries within TLF present an optimal starting point for initiating a truly participatory development process. Due to the often common background and experiences, most staff members generally have a good understanding of the problems and needs of the beneficiaries - especially those, who have formerly been beneficiaries themselves. Therefore, the brokers can comprehensively pass on the ideas of the beneficiaries about how TLF could intervene to support them to the TLF management and board. And as the organization is rooted in the community, the plans of the beneficiaries usually do not differ very much from those of TLF (this was generally confirmed in the interviews with the beneficiaries, see INT: PH, LH1, LH2; LH3).

However, although brokerage between TLF and its beneficiaries can be generally described as successful, there is one severe problem which relates to the fact that TLF often does not have the resources which would be necessary to implement what beneficiaries *and* staff have identified as viable solutions (O/ II: 11.09.; 03.09.; 10.09.). As argued in section 3.3.2, a broker can lose the trust of the beneficiaries if he/ she or his/ her organization cannot respond to their demands – no matter if this is due to irreconcilable interests of beneficiaries and organization or, as in the case of TLF, due to an inability to implement the ideas. On different occasions, I witnessed that beneficiaries expressed disappointment and frustration as promises made by TLF staff had not been kept and consequently pressurized the "TLF brokers" to do something about it (O: 17.07.; 23.07.; 30.07.; 10.09.).

On the other hand, the brokers were compelled by the organization to ensure that the beneficiaries complied with the rules and made their contribution to the programs so that these could run without disturbance. TLF employees were held to enforce discipline by sanctioning and, in severe cases, expelling those beneficiaries who were violating the rules. In this regard, the often close relations between beneficiaries and staff proved to be a hindrance and placed the broker in a difficult position (O: 24.07.; 30.07.; 06.08.; 17.08.; INT: 3, 5, 6).

All in all, one can conclude that hypotheses 2 and 3 are partially supported. However, there is also contrary evidence, namely that close relations and frequent interactions are not enough to realize participatory development (especially concerning implementation). Moreover, they can sometimes even hinder the successful realization of programs as the broker loses his authority to enforce rules and agreements upon the beneficiaries.

4.4.3 Values and Mission

In section 3.3.3 the effect of the values and the mission statement of an organization on participation and empowerment was hypothesized as following:

1. If the values and mission statements are only designed to suit funders, they may not be congruent with the beneficiaries' culture(s) and thus present an obstacle to participation.
2. If the mission of an organization is to send out professional experts to help "people with deficiencies and problems" rather than to work in partnership and provide support for the beneficiaries to realize their own "solutions", it will unlikely follow a participatory and empowering development approach. If the values of an organization center on mutual respect, partnership and cooperation, rather than primarily on technological and business-related factors, they demonstrate an organization's commitment to participation and empowerment.
3. The way an organization presents itself is an indicator of what kind of people (will) work for the organization – the more an organization portrays itself as a professional and tech-

nocratic business enterprise, the less likely it becomes that people who are committed to "soft factors" such as participation and empowerment will choose to work for the organization or will be employed by the organization.

In order to test the validity of these hypotheses one has to first look at the functions which TLF attributes to its values and mission statement. As stated in section 3.3.3.1, organizations often model their mission statements and values to suit the expectations of their funders. In this regard, TLF seems to present an exception. Although, as outlined above, TLF attempts to meet the standards set by its funders (especially concerning reports, statistics etc.), the organization strives to stay as independent as possible and does not want outsiders to interfere with its values. One informant described a case where TLF refused to compromise its values and convictions, although the funder – in that case the ILO – offered to pay large sums of money:

"[W]e do not want to change our goals to please a funder, so we never do that, we'd rather say no to the money, (…), the ILO at Lerato House is an example, they came and said 'oh, there is lots of money and we want to end child labor, so can you be on board?', but that had to be negotiated for a long time, we said we won't work with boys, number one, cause we don't and you'll have to find someone else to do that, and they wanted some specific research to be done and have certain things written about it, which would have been nice if we had the capacity, but we couldn't put one staff on the research projects, we don't have that staff capacity, so we said it will be a participatory research, us and you and the participants together seeing how we establish a model for instance in Refilwe [a former township], get that going and see the results and hear from the participants what difference that had on their lives, so there we really had to say no no no for several things, and also they wanted to give us more money, they wanted us to rescue 200 girls out of child prostitution and they would give per girl, we said before you give the money we can tell you now that we will stick to 60 or 100 and that would be our maximum that we can do, so that's the relationship" (INT: 2).

Another example of TLF refusing to succumb to funders concerns its relationship with the inner city churches. Some of these churches oppose the developmental approach which TLF has adopted and demand that TLF commits itself more strongly to missionary work and "spiritual warfare" (Krige, 2007: 93, 108f., 127). The mere concentration on proselytization, however, would not contribute to TLF's objective to help poor and vulnerable individuals and communities and foster the development of the city. One interviewee explained that TLF tries to keep the balance between evangelical and social ministry but that "the scales tip more towards the belief that you **cannot** just preach to the people" and that one has to "demonstrate God's love practically" (INT: 2).

Another function of having an established set of values and a mission statement is to create a shared culture internally. Within TLF, this seems especially important with regard to the diverse background of the staff. Knowing that everyone works for the same aim and shares common convictions helps people to believe in the idea of community and thus decreases the risk that conflicts erupt on the issues of race, faith or gender. However, rather than ignoring the differences and aiming for assimilation, TLF celebrates the inner-organizational diversity and creates opportunities for staff to share their respective cultures and discuss the differences among them, for example during the devotions or the retreat (O: 06.07.; 07.07.; 20.07.). The Christian faith serves as a particularly strong integrating factor. On several occasions it was highlighted that before God all people are the same. TLF's first value states that "[God's] redemption is sufficient to bring healing in brokenness, salvation from both personal and systemic sin [and] reconciliation in division".

The Christian belief also constitutes an important unifying element in the relations between staff and beneficiaries and for both it presents a motivating and inspiring force (INT: 3). Their faith helps staff members to endure the difficult situations they are faced with every day and gives them the strength to believe in people. As one informant explained,

"to believe in someone it has to take God working in us, to believe in someone very shabby and he hasn't bathed for the past three weeks and is smelling, for you to believe in that kind of person, you need God, so it [religion] plays a central role" (INT: 4).

The beneficiaries, most of whom are Christians (although this is not a prerequisite), appreciate the spiritual empowerment they receive from TLF (INT: LH1, LH2, LH3, PH). They are reassured by staff and told that God will redeem them, no matter what sins they have committed and no matter what problems they face (O: 11.09.; 29.08; 19.09.). All beneficiaries, even those who normally do not practice their Christianity or belong to a different faith, are strongly encouraged to attend the devotions which represent a central element of each program - this again reflecting the missionary aspect of the TLF work (INT: 5, PH, LH1, LH2; II: 26.07.).

Although being a Christian is not a prerequisite for receiving assistance from TLF, some of the informants stressed that it could lead to difficulties when beneficiaries belong to a different faith or do not practice any religion at all:

"[I]t is very difficult cause we say that all the girls must go to Melodia Tshwane [a church], first, when we admit the girl it is not an issue, but when they are here, because we do devotion with them, with all of them, and on Sunday we say they must go to church, there are instances where we had girls that were like Muslims, who would challenge…, well, what we always do is to encourage them to join us, to go with us to church, but we have never really enforced it, you know chasing you even if you don't want to, especially if you are of another religion we would rather respect that religion but say 'you know what: in this house this is our religion, so for the time being in this house can you please come with us and pray with us', but if you are just a nobody, who doesn't even show any sign of any other religious exposition, Satanist… ,that's where we really give them questions, and where we would be very very worried then" (INT: 3).

With regard to staff recruitment, having a Christian background does present an important criteria for selection, although exceptions are made – especially concerning the international volunteers. But despite practically everyone adhering to the Christian faith, religion does not always achieve to unite the staff and sometimes different convictions on what it means to be a Christian constitute reasons for conflict (II: 04.07.) as the following quotation reveals:

"[T]he criteria, we have always kind of said, one should have a background of a Christian religion, but I've seen that we should be very specific about that because we have backgrounds of various Christianity among the (…) staff, sometimes it is good cause we balance one another, but sometimes it creates clashes and problems, in terms of saying 'the way are you doing things - according to my faith you haven't done enough or we have done too much', I think the team is very much committed towards their work, and as a result all these kind of challenges we are able to work through them for the sake of the program, so I would say the team is very committed and very diverse, obviously coming from various religions, various backgrounds, various ages, various cultures" (INT: 3).

Therefore, it is important for TLF not to define its values exclusively in religious terms. Another key value which is not (primarily) religious, and which aims to unify the staff internally and to demonstrate solidarity with the beneficiaries, is the obligation to practice a simple life-style. TLF propagates that "staff members commit themselves to a simple life-style" and "will speak out against unnecessary and irresponsible consumption" (Value 11, see also TLF Policy 5.3). This presents one reason why salaries within TLF are relatively low (II: 20.07). The simple life-style exposes itself in many ways. For example, staff *and* management work in very basically designed and decorated offices, wear inexpensive clothes, and live in modest flats. The range of monthly salaries is extremely narrow when compared with other organizations and varies from 12.500 Rand for the most senior post to 1.500 Rand for the lowest ranks whereby the lower salary packages include several subsidies (Krige, 2007: 102). An informant elucidated:

"[A] simple life style, that is very important to us and that is one of our main values - a simple life style, a lot of other NGOs they just, the more money they raise, the higher their salaries can go, but I think a thing of love and care and compassion, that that is one of the main issues, is that we do this cause we love people, and that love become practical in the work, and how one conveys it, so it has a yeast effect, you do a program but the attitude is love, and that makes the difference, I really, really believe so" (INT: 2).

This attitude, however, also has severe limitations as some of the staff has to live on the verge of poverty. Two interviewees very accurately described the inherent contradictions in the TLF approach.

"You know what makes me so angry with PCM, is how we treat the PCM family, meaning the staff and their relatives and their children, (…) I feel that little is done for them, and we expect to touch the life of others outside, so it makes me angry to say, how can I go out hungry and be expected to touch a hungry soul? How can I be so broken and go out and be expected to touch someone? (…) it is so contradictory because there is also that family spirit, we are there for each other, but (…) that is where I am confused, we so much want to do things for the outside world, like for the beneficiaries (…), but the staff when they go home their life is something else, I don't know – maybe it is selfish, because for PCM to decide concentrating on their staff that would be a job of it's own…" (INT: 3)

"[B]ut the salaries (…) are low, if you are giving all your time and you are earning enough at least you will have the maid to help you wash clothes at home, to do other things, but if you are earning less you still have to struggle, you need to do it all by yourself and you cannot improve yourself, you cannot buy a car or a house for yourself, and yet you are working hard" (INT: 5).

In conclusion, one can say that the findings of the TLF case study generally confirm the above hypotheses. Although TLF is heavily dependent on external funding, it does not model its values and mission statements to please them. On the contrary, TLF has in the past even refused to accept money offered by funders if taking it would have meant to compromise its values and approach. TLF aspires to gain the trust of its beneficiaries whereby the often common background of staff and beneficiaries constitutes an important factor. The similarities between staff and beneficiaries are also reflected and even explicitly pointed out in the TLF values. In sum, this leads me to conclude that my first hypothesis is somewhat justifiable.

In accordance with the second hypothesis, one finds that TLF's mission statement ("work in partnership with churches and communities for urban transformation") and its values stress partnership, solidarity and moral principles, and that this commitment is also reflected in the organization's participatory and empowering development approach.

One can find supportive evidence for the third hypothesis as the people employed by TLF are selected according to how well they fit into the community (especially with regard to their faith). Moreover, the high staff fluctuation shows that people who are not completely dedicated to TLF's values and principles leave the organization, usually after a relatively short period of time.

4.4.4 Organizational Learning and Change
The first hypothesis regarding the *relevance* of learning for an organization (with regard to implementing participation and empowerment) which was developed in section 3.3.4 stated:

The less the original (founding) values, concepts and approaches of an organization are focused on participation and empowerment, the less likely it is that the organization will promote "true" participatory and empowering development, also in the long run.

As I have repeatedly pointed out, TLF's founding values, concepts and approaches are very much in favor of and compatible with participatory and empowering development. However, section 4.4.1 has revealed that processes of professionalization and bureaucratization have started to have detrimental effects on TLF's approach to participation and empowerment and that this trend will probably continue in the future. It seems probable but remains to be seen to what extent TLF will forfeit its participatory and empowering approach in order to adapt to the institutional system and become more influential. Therefore, one cannot conclusively assess the above hypothesis with regard to the case of TLF.

In the following section I will thus concentrate on the second hypothesis concerning organizational learning which reads:

The more an organization is endowed with mechanisms to change and/ or possesses structural features that allow for learning and change, the higher are the chances that the organization can react to (new) trends in development cooperation (e.g. participation), integrate new research findings and alter its underlying concepts.

I will analyze whether one can speak of TLF as a learning organization and, if yes, how learning takes place. I will furthermore reflect on how processes of learning and change within TLF affect the organization's approach to participation and empowerment.

The most important factor affecting organizational learning relates to an organization's perceptual frames and philosophy or, to put it more simply, the question whether an organization "wants" to and is endowed with mechanisms to learn. With regard to the first question, it is therefore compelling to analyze the attitude of TLF towards learning. Several indicators suggest that learning represents a central objective of TLF, above all the organization's openness for criticism, feedback and evaluation both from the outside and from within.

TLF receives **external feedback** from funders, advisory groups as well as from partnering institutions (INT: 2, 3, 6). A systematic external evaluation was conducted in 2000 and, according to the director, should be repeated on a regular basis (Krige, 2007: 78). The unexceptional openness of TLF towards external feedback reveals itself in the fact that two researchers (Skip Krige and myself) were granted the permission to analyze the organization and were given virtually unrestricted access to meetings, workshops, documents and all sorts of informal information. The sole benefit which resulted for the organization from the research (on which TLF had no influence) was to receive a critical feedback. Throughout my research, I was encouraged on several occasions to be critical and evaluate the working processes within TLF as an "outsider" (O/ II: 17.07.; 29.08.; 17.09.; 19.09.; 20.09.).

Internal evaluation has, to put it in Krige's words, "become a lifestyle" (2007: 78) within TLF. During meetings, devotions, and on the retreats staff can voice concerns and express ideas for change; reports, written feedbacks and individual consultations also serve as important instruments to disclose the opinion of staff (O/ II: 30.08.; 10.09.; 17.09.; 19.09.). Furthermore, TLF makes an effort to assess and consider criticisms and suggestions of the beneficiaries. An especially valuable contribution to the learning process is the feedback of former beneficiaries who have profited from the support of TLF, as the following quotation reveals:

"[W]ith people who have lived in Potter's House and now they are working for PCM (…), what we want to do is learn from them now, we want to do what we call a Potter's House reunion, whereby we have a day where we are calling all of the ex-Potter's House to come, and where we share what was good that supported you and helped you to come out of your situation, now you are working, now you are housemother, now you are a receptionist, what is it that lifted you? How do you think we can help others that are coming now? What can you also help us?" (INT: 5).

Another important indicator of TLF being a learning organization relates to the organization's concept of staff development which entails that every employee (including every volunteer) should participate in trainings and workshops on a regular basis (Policy 1.11/ 14). This reflects the belief that organizational learning and change can only occur when the individual members of the organization are given the chance to learn and develop themselves. As one informant maintained: "PCM – it is one organization where you do a lot of learning, I think there is more space for people to learn" (INT: 4). Another informant confirmed that for a social and development organization like TLF it was of utmost importance to "be a learning organization, to learn as an organization how to do the work better and better all the time, but staff also improving their skills, and even experience, like being exposed to other ministries and other countries and places, and spiritual growth as well, maturity" (INT: 2).

One can conclude that an aspiration to learn and constantly adapt to changing challenges constitutes a central part of TLF's philosophy. On the other hand, the organization also wants to convey its ideas and knowledge to others and hence engages in mutual "learning and teaching processes". Staff, volunteers, and beneficiaries, for example, come to TLF to learn and develop themselves, but at the same time the organization relies heavily on their input and their experiences (INT: 3, 4, 5, 7). In its dealings with the City Council and local government, TLF has to adapt to their standards and directives, but at the same time TLF challenges them on many issues and thus also influences the development of Tshwane (INT: 2, 4, 6). Another example of mutual learning relates to the managing director of TLF: in his sermons and his decisions regarding TLF he relies on theological and sociological publications and studies (INT: 2; O: 13.07.; 17.08.; 14.09.); at the same time he contributes to the social-scientific discourses and has published a number of articles and papers which reflect his practical experiences (Krige, 2007: 79f.).

After having established that one can speak of TLF as a learning organization, I will now briefly assess how learning within the organization takes places with reference to the concepts introduced in section 3.3.4. "Learning by exploring" which entails experimenting and taking risks, is the concept which best describes TLF's approach to learning. One of TLF's values states: **"We value risk. We call for pioneer ministries into new areas of need and opportunity. We call for bold and creative ministry initiatives..."** TLF's institutional history as depicted in section 4.1.1 reflects the organization's explorative learning process and its unique constitution and position in the organizational landscape of Tshwane. As the organization institutionalizes, learning occurs less frequently by exploring and is instead replaced by the concept of "learning by doing", which characterizes learning processes based on routine in a stable environment. Evidently, TLF has also learned "by doing" and "by imitating". The Leadership Foundation model, which underlies TLF's structure and conceptual framework, for example, was developed in the USA and has, since the 1990s, expanded to a small number of cities around the world (Krige, 2007: 34ff.).

Relating back to the concept of single and double loop learning, one can posit that most of the learning attempts of TLF are directed at improving the work effectiveness (and efficiency) and are thus "single loop". Examples include the change of programs to better suit the beneficiaries' needs, the empowerment of staff through training to enable them to better accomplish their work, or the reliance on the knowledge of volunteers (or other experts) to install new technologies. Double loop learning, entailing a modification of norms and values, is much harder to identify. One could argue that in the process of professionalization and bureaucratization, TLF is undergoing a change of its norms and values (see section 4.4.1) as the organization has to sacrifice some elements of its central value "community" in order to become more professional and efficient (as defined by bureaucratic standards). With regard to participation, this would entail a change towards the negative because, as demonstrated, TLF's approach to participation and empowerment is indivisibly linked to the organization's idea of being a community of staff and beneficiaries.

Lastly, I will now go back to the second hypothesis. As shown, TLF is endowed with several mechanisms for change. But has this led TLF to incorporate (new) research findings and theoretical concepts, especially with regard to participation and empowerment? To answer this question I refer to the study of Krige (2007) who has systematically evaluated TLF according to selected faith-based and non-faith-based development approaches and theories[63]. Most of these approaches center on principles which are crucial to the idea of participatory and empowering development. These principles include, among others, a commitment to holism, sustainability, capacity-building, self-reliance, ownership, transformation as well as to asset-based, community-based and community-driven development. Krige concludes that TLF successfully applies, and has over the years increased, its understanding of the theories and approaches analyzed. In his final analysis he maintains that

"it is clear that it [TLF] has a comprehensive understanding of a faith-based [and non-faith-based] developmental approach and is applying associated principles in its operations, consisting of spiritual, institutional, methodological, social, economic, political, and environmental elements. (...) Holistic empowerment is at the heart of the TLF approach, which practices empowering others and at the same time being empowered by others at all levels. Impressive advancements have been made over the last few years in terms of spirituality, increasing institutional capacity, expanding scope and influence, and engagement with civil society" (Krige, 2007: 134).

Krige's analysis leads me to conclude that TLF has made use of its learning capacities in that it has applied influential concepts and theories currently discussed in the context of participatory development. From my own experience, I can recount that TLF continues to integrate research findings into its work and uses these to adapt, refine and improve its development approach. Therefore, the second hypothesis seems compelling when applied to the case of TLF. The chances are high that the organization will be able to react to new trends in participatory development – also in the future.

4.4.5 Concluding Reflections – the Contradictions of Participatory Development

I will now briefly summarize and interpret the insights which were gained by applying the four concepts developed in section 3.3 to the case of TLF by pointing out two "contradictions" of participatory and empowering development. These may not only be of relevance in the case of TLF but may, at least to some extent, be generalizable across the wider field of development cooperation.

The first contradiction relates to the fact that organizations have to professionalize and institutionalize in order to become influential and gain access to

---

[63] These include alternative development, asset-based community development, social movement theory (according to Korten), and several faith-based development approaches.

larger (financial) resources which they need to advance their objectives. As soon as they do, however, they seem to automatically become less participatory and empowering because they employ "experts" rather than people from the community, introduce hierarchies and standardize procedures and end up taking decisions "top-down" rather than "bottom-up".

The second contradiction is closely linked to the first. It appears that those organizations which have large resources and qualified, professional staff, have huge difficulties in working in a participatory manner, especially in the planning phase, which is at least partly due to the often huge social, educational and cultural differences between the experts and the beneficiaries. A common criticism voiced against these organizations is that they are too "patronizing" and thus do not achieve to initiate a sustainable and independent development process which is managed by the (empowered) beneficiaries. On the other hand, smaller and less professional organizations such as TLF, which are very close to their beneficiaries and therefore follow an inherently participatory approach, sometimes lack important resources and/ or skills. These would be necessary to successfully *implement* the ideas which were generated through participatory measures in the planning phase. As I have demonstrated for the case of TLF, this presented one of the main reasons why the organization could not follow up and realize many of their plans.

These identified contradictions and complexities, summarized in table 3, in fact strengthen the argument of development critiques who stress that the inherent mechanisms of international development cooperation prevent that development can ever be truly participatory and empowering.

Type of Organization	Planning Phase	Implementation Phase
Large (international) organizations with highly qualified staff and substantial resources	- superficial participation - no real understanding of beneficiaries' living circumstances and of their problems and needs	- many resources to implement projects - highly skilled staff can put the ideas and plans into practice
Smaller (local) organizations with (mainly) local staff and fewer resources	- very participatory (inherently) - (most) staff have a thorough understanding of beneficiaries' living situations, and can therefore better comprehend their needs	- Lack of resources and skills to implement the ideas which were identified in a partici-patory manner during the planning phase

Table 3: Complexity of Participatory Development

5. Synthesis

Since the beginning of the 1990s, participatory development constitutes one of the major paradigms within the field of development. However, social scientists have pointed out several shortcomings in the implementation of the approach. One central point of criticism relates to the cultures and structures of development organizations. The aim of this M.A. thesis was to systematically explore the influence of organizational culture on participation and empowerment. Two principle questions were raised:

1. How does the organizational culture of a development organization influence the way it implements participation and empowerment?
2. What general inferences emerge from the systematic analysis of question 1 for the study and practical application of participatory development?

In order to answer these questions, I adopted a twofold approach and structured my work accordingly: the first part comprises theoretical reflections on how to model the relationship between the two variables – organizational culture and participatory development. Derived from a thorough literature review, I developed four concepts and a total of nine working hypotheses which I then applied to the case-study of an organization involved in social and development work – the Tshwane Leadership Foundation. The case study presents the second major part of my M.A. thesis.

The main conclusion to be drawn from this study is that organizational culture seems to have a large effect on how an organization functions and thus also on what kind of approach it adopts towards participation and empowerment. In the following paragraphs, I will present the findings of my research in more detail with regard to the two questions outlined above.

Responding to question 1, one can first state that four aspects of an organization's culture – the degree of professionalism, the way in which the staff members fulfill their role as development brokers, the values and mission the organization propagates and its ability to learn - influence the approach an organization adopts towards participation and empowerment.

Concerning the first aspect, an organization's degree of professionalism, the case study of TLF generally confirms what has been suggested in other organizational studies: in the process of professionalizing, organizations seem to gradually install a top-down bureaucracy, establish clear(er) hierarchies and sacrifice some of their original objectives and ideals in order to become more influential. TLF, currently in a state of insetting professionalization, exposed some of these trends, the most evident being a formalization of processes and staff affairs, an increase in bureaucracy and some changes in the organization's original values. These developments pose threats to TLF's unique community development model which is hitherto also the foundation of the organization's approach to participation and empowerment.

On a more general level, the evidence from theory and case study has led me to infer that the more professional and bureaucratic an organization is or becomes, the more difficulties it will face in establishing and/ or maintaining close relationships to its beneficiaries and grassroots supporters and thus in rendering the development process participatory and empowering.

As a second aspect, I assessed the role of the staff in facilitating participation and empowerment with reference to the concept of "development brokers" (see Mosse/ Lewis, 2006). Concerning organizational culture, this is of relevance because the behavior of the individual staff members is always dependent on the characteristics/ culture of the organization they work for. Through the case study analysis, I tried to demonstrate that successful participation and empowerment of beneficiaries is determined, at least to some extent, by the skillfulness *as well as* the willingness and commitment of the broker, who passes on their opinions and suggestions to higher levels in the organization. A high congruence between the cultures of broker, beneficiaries and organization as well as frequent mutual exchanges between all stakeholders increase the probability of successful brokerage. However, the analysis of TLF revealed that cultural proximity and frequent interactions can sometimes also present an impediment as the broker may lose the authority to enforce decisions, rules and agreements.

A third indicator of an organization's culture *and* its approach to participation and empowerment are its values and mission-statement. The more these are intended to please the funders rather than the beneficiaries of the organization, the less likely it is that the organization will be able to successfully implement participation and empowerment. TLF probably presents a notable exception to other organizations in that it does not let funders gain influence on its values, missions and proceedings and rather aspires to win the trust of its beneficiaries by stressing the similarities between staff and beneficiaries. This has positive effects on the participation and empowerment processes within TLF.

Values which center on respect, partnership and cooperation rather than efficiency and effectiveness seem more congruent with participatory development. It remains questionable, however, whether organizations which stress these "participatory attributes" really transmit their "rhetorical commitment" to their practical work. At least for the case of TLF, one can state that the values and mission it proclaims (and which reveal an obligation to participatory principles) in actual fact reflect the way the organization tackles participation and empowerment in practice.

A further function of value- and mission-statements is to convey a certain image of the organization to outsiders and potential employees. The values may serve as a first indicator for a job applicant as to whether he/ she shares the beliefs and principles of the organization. Conversely, an organization will select applicants according to how well they harmonize with the organizational culture. TLF is a case in point. The organization strives to employ only those people who fit into the "community". On the other hand, those employees who do not feel sufficiently dedicated to TLF's values and principles usually leave the organization after a relatively short period of time. With regard to participation and empowerment, one can deduce that if an organization convincingly presents itself as participatory and community-based, the chances are high that job applicants will also be committed to these values (which again is essential for the successful realization of participatory development as has already been pointed out above).

The fourth concept proved the most difficult to assess in the case study. The literature on institutional theory suggests that the founding norms, ideas and rules of an organization have a long-lasting impact on its development. However, it would really take a long-term study to systematically analyze how far the founding values impede an organization from adopting new paradigms. The case study of TLF does not give enough information about this matter. With regard to participation and empowerment, I nonetheless suppose that the less the original values, concepts and approaches of an organization are congruent with participation and empowerment, the less likely it is that the organization can and will adopt a truly participatory approach. The current state of development affairs seems to provide ample evidence.

What one can postulate from the case study of TLF is that the ability of an organization to learn affects the extent to which it incorporates new concepts and research findings (e.g. on participatory development) into its work. TLF is an organization profoundly endowed with mechanisms which encourage/ allow for learning and change and has over the years succeeded in integrating current research findings, theories and principles of development into its work as has been demonstrated by Krige (2007). In the long run, I believe that it is the ability of development organization to learn which will essentially determine whether the reforms necessary to improve the current state of participatory development will take place, or whether participatory development will become just another development paradigm soon to be replaced.

The reflections on utilizing the concept of organizational learning to explain the difficulties an organization may face in implementing participatory development lead me to my second question: What can be drawn from the insights hitherto discussed for the theoretical debate as well as the practice of (participatory) development?

In the continuous debates on the merits and weaknesses of participatory development, several points of criticism have been pointed out which relate to the methods and principles by which development organizations have tried to implement participatory development. These debates have led to gradual changes in development practices. Formerly, participation was regarded mainly as a way to enhance the efficiency of projects. Today, it is widely accepted that extensive participation and empowerment of the "marginalized" are necessary to render development efforts sustainable and tackle the underlying causes of poverty and exclusion. However, there are still major problems which obstruct the successful implementation of participatory development: a "mythical" conception of community, difficulties in identifying legitimate representatives of the target group, a focus on the methods and techniques of participation while ignoring the importance of political factors and context, an underestimation of the necessity of structural change and/ or the conflict potential that comes with it, and lastly, the bureaucratic structure of the development system.

Most of the attempts to improve the current state of development have centered on the creation of new methods, paradigms and approaches. It seems, however, that one central factor has hitherto been largely ignored, namely that one of the central constraints of development lies in the organizations which are to implement it. The necessity to concentrate on the structures and cultures of development organization has been demonstrated throughout this work and presents one important contribution to the discourse. Concerning the debates on participatory development, a comparative strength of the study lies in its systematic focus on the internal factors of an organization and how these affect participatory development.

A further insight which can be drawn from the study confirms the suppositions of many development critiques; namely, that there are certain structural constraints inherent in the concept of development and development cooperation which conflict with the principles of participation and empowerment and which hinder the realization of the benefits associated with these concepts.

The most fundamental problem relates to the fact that development cooperation works according to the principles of a market economy and this does not always go hand in hand with the principles of charity. As an example, one can look at the criteria which decide whether an organization can gain influence and respect in the international field of development which is necessary in order to receive funding. It appears that attributes such as professionalism and efficiency as well as a support of a "western" approach to development are considered more important than "soft factors" such as a close relationship to the target group and a long-term and culturally adapted approach to development. With regard to the paradigm of participation, this evidently leads to a fundamental problem. Large, influential and professionally equipped development organizations are not suited to implement participatory development despite the huge resources and highly skilled experts available to them. This is due to the fact that their working approaches, principles and concepts are too distant from those of the beneficiaries they wish to serve. The "experts" do not share common experiences with the beneficiaries, cannot really comprehend their problems, needs and living circumstances, and thus cannot take these fully into account when planning and designing a project. This severely hinders participation and empowerment.

Less prominent organizations, on the other hand, which operate on a smaller scale and have fewer resources, face a different problem with regard to participatory development. They are usually much closer to the "grassroots" and therefore better understand what their beneficiaries require. However, they often lack the resources and skilled personnel which would be necessary to implement the ideas and demands voiced by the beneficiaries.

My concluding statement brings me back to what I have already acknowledged in the introduction: development is full of contradictions, ambivalences and paradoxes. This holds true for participatory development all the more and leads me to a rather pessimistic outlook on the realization of the (theoretically) large potentials of this approach on a broad scale.

The aim of this study has not been to give precise recommendations on how development organizations can better adapt to the requirements of true participatory development. This presents an objective for future research. A further limitation of the study is that it is unclear whether the insights gained from the case study of one particular organization – the Tshwane Leadership Foundation - can be generalized across the vast scope of development organizations; especially since TLF adheres to a fairly unconventional development approach. More studies of different types of organizations, operating in different settings would therefore be necessary.

However, the analysis and reflections presented in the preceding pages serve as a primary reference point for contemplating how inner-organizational characteristics constrain the implementation of participation and empowerment. Although I have emphasized the complexities and contradictions of participatory development, I do not wish to suggest that one should refrain from propagating the approach which unmistakably comprises many advantages. What I do want to emphasize is that in the current system of development it is not surprising that many of these advantages have not been exploited.

In his essay "Paradoxes of Participation", Cleaver (1999: 608) states that "[t]here is a need for a radical reassessment of the desirability, practicality and efficacy of development efforts based on community participation. This involves not just rethinking the relationship between differently placed individuals and historically and spatially specific social structures, but also the role of individuals, households, communities, development agencies and the state".

It remains to be seen whether one day the contradictions, ambivalences and paradoxes of (participatory) development will be overcome. For the moment, I am skeptical...

83

6. REFERENCES

Aarre, Karen. 1998. The Child Welfare Debate in Portugal: a Case Study of a Children's Home. In: Edgar, Iain R. and Russel, Andrew (eds.). 1998. The Anthropology of Welfare. London/ New York: Routledge. (57-72).

Acre, Alberto and Long, Norman. 1993. Bridging Two Worlds: an Ethnography of Bureaucrat – Peasant Relations in Western Mexico. In: Hobart, Mark (ed.). 1993. An Anthropological Critique of Development – The Growth of Ignorance. London/ New York: Routledge. (179-208).

Agrawal, Arun and Gibson, Clark C. 1999. Entchantment and Disentchantment: The Role of Community in Natural Ressource Management. In: World Development, Vol. 27, No. 4. (629-649).

Antweiler, Christoph. 2002. Ethnologie und Ethik: Praxisrelevante Grundlagendebatten. In: Bliss, Frank, Schönhuth, Michael and Zucker, Petra (eds.). 2002. Welche Ethik braucht die Entwicklungszusammenarbeit? Beiträge zur Kulturkunde, Bd. 22. Bonn: PAS. (25-49).

Arbeitsgemeinschaft Entwicklungsethnologie (AGEE). 2002. Ethnische Leitlinien der AGEE: Erläuterungen und Praxishinweise. In: Bliss, Frank, Schönhuth, Michael and Zucker, Petra (eds.). 2002. Welche Ethik braucht die Entwicklungszusammenarbeit? Beiträge zur Kulturkunde, Bd. 22. Bonn: PAS. (169-201).

Argyris, Chris and Schön, Donald A. 1996. Organizational Learning II – Theory, Method and Practice. Reading, MA: Addison-WesleyPublishing Company.

Arnold, Guy. 1996. Historical Dictionary of Aid and Development Organizations. International Organizations Series, No. 10. Lanham, Md./ London: The Scarecrow Press.

Bargatzky, Thomas. 1997. Ethnologie – Eine Einführung in die Wissenschaft von den urproduktiven Gesellschaften. Hamburg: Helmut Buske Verlag.

Bebbington, Anthony. 2004. Theorizing Participation and Institutional Change: Ethnography and Political Economy. In: Hickey, Sam and Mohan, Giles (eds.). 2004. Participation – From Tyranny to Transformation? Exploring New Approaches to Participation in Development. London/ New York: Zed Books. (278-283).

Beckmann, Gabriele. 1997. Partizipation in der Entwicklungszusammenarbeit – Mode, Methode oder politische Vision? Hamburg: LIT Verlag.

Beer, Bettina. 2003. Einleitung: Feldforschungsmethoden. In: Beer, B. (ed.): Methoden und Techniken der Feldforschung. Berlin: Dietrich Reimer Verlag. (9-33).

Bernard, Russel. 2002. Research Methods in Anthropology. Qualitative and Quantitative Approaches. 3. Edition. Walnut Creek, CA: AltaMira Press.

Beyer, Janice M. and Trice, Harrison M. 1988. The Communication of Power Relations in Organizations through Cultural Rites. In: Jones, Michael O., Moore, Michael D. and Snyder, Richard C. (eds.). 1988. Inside Organizations – Understanding the Human Dimension. Newsbury Park/ London/ New Delhi: Sage Publications. (141-158).

Bierschenk, Thomas and de Sardan, Olivier. 2003. Powers in the Village: Rural Benin Between Democratization and Decentralization. In: Africa, Vol. 73, No. 2. (145-173).

Blaikie, Piers. 2006. Is Small Really Beautiful? Community-based Natural Ressource Management in Malawi and Botswana. In: World Development, Vol. 34, No. 11. (1942-1957).

Bliss, Frank. 1996. „Participatory Appraisals" – Anmerkungen zu einem Mythos. In: Bliss, Frank and Neumann, Stefan (eds.). 1996. Ethnologische Beiträge zur Entwicklungspolitik. Bonn: PAS. (52-64).

Bliss, Frank and Neumann, Stefan. 2006. Partizipation - Ungefragt beteiligt. In: E+Z, Vol. 47, No. 11. (424-425).

Botes, Lucius and Van Rensburg, Dingie. 2000. Community Participation in Development: Nine Plagues and Twelve Commandments. In: Community Development Journal, Vol. 35, No. 1. (40-58).

Carothers, Thomas. 1999. Aiding Democracy Abroad – The Learning Curve. Washington D.C.: Carnegie Endowment for International Peace.

Carothers, Thomas and Ottaway, Marina. 2000. The Burgeoning World of Civil Society Aid/ Towards Civil Society Realism. In: Carothers, Thomas and Ottaway, Marina (eds.). 2000. Funding Virtues – Civil Society Aid and Democracy Promotion. Washington, D.C.: Carnegie Endowment for International Peace. (3-21/ 293-310).

Chambers, Robert. 1997. Whose Reality Counts? Putting the First Last. London: Intermediate Technology Publications.

Chambers, Robert. 1994. Participatory Rural Appraisals (PRA): Challenges, Potentials and Paradigm. In: World Development, Vol. 22, No. 10. (1437-1454).

Chinsinga, Blessings. 2003. The Participatory Development Approach under a Microscope: the Case of the Poverty Alleviation Programme in Malawi. In: Journal of Social Development in Africa, Vol. 18, No. 1. (129-144).

Cleaver, Frances. 2007. Institutions, Agency and the Limitations of Participatory Approaches to Development. In: Cooke, Bill and Kothari, Uma (eds.). 2007 (4th impression). Participation: The new Tyranny? London/ New York: Zed Books. (36-55).

Cleaver, Frances. 1999. Paradoxes of Participation: Questioning Participatory Approaches to Development. In. Journal of International Development: 11. (597-612).

Cowen, Micheal P. and Shenton, Robert W. 1996. Doctrines of Development. London/ New York: Routledge.

Cooke, Bill and Kothari, Uma (eds.). 2007 (4th impression). Participation: The new Tyranny? London/ New York: Zed Books.

Cooke, Bill and Kothari, Uma. 2007. The Case for Participation as Tyranny. In: Cooke, Bill and Kothari, Uma (eds.). 2007 (4th impression). Participation: The new Tyranny? London/ New York: Zed Books. (1-15).

Cornwall, Andrea. 2003. Whose Voices? Whose Choices? Reflections on Gender and Participatory Development. In: World Development, Vol. 31, No. 8. (1325-1342).

Cornwall, Andrea. 2002. Beneficiary, Consumer, Citizen: Perspectives on Participation for Poverty Reduction. SIDA Studies No. 2/ 21.

Crewe, Emma and Harrison, Elizabeth. 1998. Whose Development? An Ethnography of Aid. London/ New York: Zed Books.

Dannhaeuser, Norbert and Werner, Cynthia. 2003. Introduction. In: Dannhaeuser, Norbert and Werner, Cynthia (eds.). 2003. Anthropological Perspectives on Economic Development and Integration. Research in Economic Anthropology, Vol. 22. Oxford: ELSEVIER. (xi-xxv).

Deal, Terrence, E. and Kennedy, Allan, A. 1982. Corporate Cultures. The Rites and Rituals of Corporate Life. Reading, MA: Addison Wesley.

Diel-Khalil, Helga and Götz, Klaus. 1999. Ethnologie und Organisationsentwicklung. Zweite, durchgesehene und erweiterte Auflage. München, Mering: Rainer Hampp Verlag.

Douglas, Mary. 1987. How Institutions Think. London: Routledge and Keagan Paul.

Eberlei, Walter. 2003. Partizipation und Ownership in den PRS – Zu wenig Zivilgesellschaft, zu viel Weltbank. In: E+Z, Vol. 44, No. 11. (411-413).

Ebrahim, Alnoor. 2003. NGOs and Organizational Change: Discourse, Reporting, and Learning. Cambridge: Cambridge University Press.

Edwards, Jeanette. 1994. Idioms of Bureaucracy and Informality in a Local Housing Aid Office. In: Wright, Susan (ed.). 1994. Anthropology of Organizations. London/ New York: Routledge. (196-209).

Eyben, Rosalind. 2000. Development and Anthropology: a View from Inside the Agency. In: Critique of Anthropology. Vol. 20, No. 1. (7-14).

Finsterbusch, Kurt and Van Wicklin III, Warren. 1989. Beneficiary Participation in Development Projects: Empirical Tests of Popular Theories. In: Economic Development and Cultural Change. Vol. 37, No. 3. (573-593).

Fischer, Hans and Beer, Bettina (eds.). 2006. Ethnologie – Einführung und Überblick. 6. überarbeitete Auflage. Berlin: Dietrich Reimer Verlag.

Francis, Paul. 2007. Participatory Development at the World Bank: the Primary of the Process. In: Cooke, Bill and Kothari, Uma (eds.). 2007 (4th impression). Participation: The new Tyranny? London/ New York: Zed Books. (72-87).

Frantz, Christiane. 2005. Karriere in NGOs – Politik als Beruf jenseits der Parteien. Wiesbaden: Verlag für Sozialwissenschaften.

Franzpötter, Reiner. 1997. Organisationskultur: Begriffsverständnis und Analyse aus interpretativ-soziologischer Sicht. Baden-Baden: Nomos Verlagsgesellschaft.

Freire, Paulo. 1971. Pädagogik der Unterdrückten. Stuttgart/ Berlin: Kreuz-Verlag.

Friedman, John T. 2006. Beyond the Post-Structural Impasse in the Anthropology of Development. In: Dialectical Anthropology, Vol. 30, No. 3-4. (201-225).

87

Gaventa, John. 2004. Towards Participatory Governance: Assessing the Transformative Possibilities. In: Hickey, Sam and Mohan, Giles (eds.). 2004. Participation – From Tyranny to Transformation? Exploring New Approaches to Participation in Development. London/ New York: Zed Books. (25-41).

Gerring, John. 2004. What is a Case Study and What is it Good for? In: American Political Science Review. Vol. 98, No. 2. (341-354).

Götz, Sabine. 1997. Unternehmenskultur – Die Arbeitswelt einer Großbäckerei aus kulturwissenschaftlicher Sicht. Münster, New York et al.: Waxmann.

Grillo, Ralph D. 1997. Discourses of Development: The view from Anthropology. In: Grillo, Ralph D and Stirrat, Roderick L.(eds.). 1997. Discourses of Development. Anthropological Perspectives. Oxford/ New York: Berg (1-34).

Hailey, John. 2007. Beyond the Formulaic: Process and Practice in South Asian NGOs. In: Cooke, Bill and Kothari, Uma (eds.). 2007 (4th impression). Participation: The new Tyranny? London/ New York: Zed Books. (88-101).

Hall, Peter A. and Taylor, Rosemary C. 1996. Political Science and the Three New Institutionalisms. In: Political Studies. Vol. 44, No. 5. (936-951).

Hamada, Tomoko. 1994. Anthropology and Organizational Culture. In: Hamada, Tomoko and Sibley, Willis E. (eds.). 1994. Anthropological Perspectives on Organizational Culture. Lanham/ New York/ London: University Press of America. (3-56).

Hauser-Schäublin, Brigitta. 2003. Teilnehmende Beobachtung. In: Beer, Bettina (ed.). 2003. Methoden und Techniken der Feldforschung. Berlin: Dietrich Reimer Verlag. (33-55).

Hayer, Maarten A. 1993. Discourse Coalitions and the Institutionalization of Practice: The Case of Acid Rain in Britain. In: Fischer, Frank and Forester, John (eds.). 1993. The Argumentative Turn in Policy Analysis and Planning. Durham/ London: Duke University Press. (43-76).

Helmers, Sabine. 1993. Zur Einführung. In: Helmers, Sabine (ed.). 1993. Ethnologie der Arbeitswelt – Beispiele aus europäischen und außereuropäischen Feldern. Bonn: Holos Verlag. (7-10).

Helmers, Sabine (ed.). 1993. Ethnologie der Arbeitswelt – Beispiele aus europäischen und außereuropäischen Feldern. Bonn: Holos Verlag.

Henkel, Heiko and Stirrat, Roderick. 2007. Participation as Spiritual Duty; Empowerment as Secular Subjection. In: Cooke, Bill and Kothari, Uma (eds.). 2007 (4th impression). Participation: The new Tyranny? London/ New York: Zed Books. (168-184).

Hickey, Sam and Mohan, Giles[1] (eds.). 2004. Participation – From Tyranny to Transformation? Exploring New Approaches to Participation in Development. London/ New York: Zed Books.

Hickey, Sam and Mohan, Giles[2]. 2004. Towards Participation as Transformation: Critical Themes and Challenges. In: Hickey, Sam and Mohan, Giles (eds.). 2004. Participation – From Tyranny to Transformation? Exploring New Approaches to Participation in Development. London/ New York: Zed Books. (3-24).

Hickey, Sam and Mohan, Giles[3]. 2004. Relocating Participation within a Radical Politics of Development: Insights from Political Action and Practice. In: Hickey, Sam and Mohan, Giles (eds.). 2004. Participation – From Tyranny to Transformation? Exploring New Approaches to Participation in Development. London/ New York: Zed Books. (159-174).

Hirsch, Eric and Gellner, David N. 2001. Introduction: Ethnography of Organizations and Organizations of Ethnography. In: Gellner, David N. and Hirsch, Eric (eds.). 2001. Inside Organizations – Anthropologists at Work. Oxford/ New York: Berg. (1-18).

Hirsch, Eric and Gellner, David N. (eds.). 2001. Inside Organizations – Anthropologists at Work. Oxford/ New York: Berg.

Hobart, Mark. 1993. Introduction: the Growth of Ignorance? In: Hobart, Mark (ed.). 1993. An Anthropological Critique of Development – The Growth of Ignorance. London/ New York: Routledge. (1-30).

Hodson, Randy. 2004. A Meta-Analysis of Workplace Ethnographies: Race, Gender, and Employee Attitudes and Behaviors. In: Journal of Contemporary Ethnography. Vol. 33, No. 1. (4-38).

Hoggett, Paul. 1987. Going beyond a Rearrangement of the Deckchairs: some Practical Hints for Councilors and Managers. In: Hoggett, Paul and Hambleton, Robin (eds.). 1987. Decentralization and Democracy: Locating Public Services. School of Advanced Urban Studies Occasional Paper No. 28. Bristol: University of Bristol. (157-167).

89

Holland, Jeremy; Brocklesby, Mary Ann and Abugre, Charles. 2004. Beyond the Technical Fix? Participation in Donor Approaches to Rights-Based Development. In: Hickey, Sam and Mohan, Giles (eds.). 2004. Participation – From Tyranny to Transformation? Exploring New Approaches to Participation in Development. London/ New York: Zed Books. (252-268).

Hutson, Susan and Liddiard, Mark. 1993. Agencies and Young People – Runaways and Young Homeless in Wales. In: Pottier, Johan (ed.). 1993. Practicing Development – Social Science Perspectives. London: Routledge. (34-49).

Isaacs, Anita. 2000. International Assistance for Democracy – A Cautionary Tale. In: Dominguez, Jorge. 2000. The Future of Inter-American Relations. New York/ London: Routledge. (259-286).

Jones, Michael O., Moore, Michael D. and Snyder, Richard C. (eds.). 1988. Inside Organizations – Understanding the Human Dimension. Newsbury Park/ London/ New Delhi: Sage Publications.

Jordan, Brigitte and Dalal, Brinda. 2006. Persuasive Encounters: Ethnography in the Corporation. In: Field Methods, Vol. 18, No. 4. (359-381).

Kievelitz, Uwe. 1996. Partizipation, soziale Prozesse und „Empowerment": Kommentare und Ergänzungen zum Artikel von Michael Schönhuth. In: Bliss, Frank and Neumann, Stefan (eds.). 1996. Ethnologische Beiträge zur Entwicklungspolitik. Bonn: PAS. (37-51).

Kilby, Patrick. 2006. Accountability for Empowerment: Dilemmas facing Non-Governmental Organizations. In: World Development, Vol. 34, No. 6. (951-963).

Korten, David, C. 1990. Getting to the 21st Century – Voluntary Action and the Global Agenda. Connecticut: Kumarian Press.

Krige, Skip. 2007. The Quest for a Faith-Based Development Approach in an African City Context based on the Tshwane Leadership Foundation Experience. Bloemfontain: University of the Free State. (unpublished mini-dissertation).

Krummacher, André. 2004. Der Participatory Rural Appraisal (PRA)-Ansatz aus ethnologischer Sicht. PRA – a quick and dirty anthropology? Arbeitspapiere Nr. 36 (ed. Bierschenk, Thomas). Mainz: Institut für Ethnologie und Afrikastudien, Johannes Gutenberg-Universität.

Kruip, Gerhard. 2007. Introduction. In: Kruip, Gerhard and Reifeld, Helmut (eds.). 2007. Church and Civil Society – The Role of Christian Churches in the Emerging Countries of Argentina, Mexico, Nigeria and South Africa. Sankt Augustin/ Berlin: Konrad Adenauer Stiftung. (11-18).

Lang, Hartmut. 1994. Wissenschaftstheorie für die ethnologische Praxis. Zweite, vollständige überarbeitete und erweiterte Auflage. Berlin: Dietrich Reimer Verlag.

Lister, Sarah. 2003. NGO Legitimacy: Technical issue or Social Construct? In: Critique of Anthropology, Vol. 23, No. 2. (175-192).

Lloyd, Peter. 1998. Residents' Participation in the Management of Retirement Housing in the UK. In: Edgar, Iain R. and Russel, Andrew (eds.). 1998. The Anthropology of Welfare. London/ New York: Routledge. (228-245).

Mansuri, Ghazala and Rao, Vijayendra. 2004. Community-Based and –Driven Development: a Critical Review. In: The World Bank Research Observer, Vol. 19, No.1. (1-39).

Mansuri, Ghazala and Rao, Vijayendra. 2003. Evaluating Community-Based and Community-Driven Development: A Critical Review of the Evidence. World Bank: Development Research Group.

March, James. 1999. The Pursuit of Organizational Intelligence. Oxford: Blackwell Publishers Ltd.

Martens, Kerstin. 2006. Institutionalizing Societal Activism within Global Governance Structures: Amnesty International and the United Nations System. In: Journal of International Development and Development, Vol. 9, No. 4. (371-395).

Martin, Joanna; Frost, Peter and O'Neill, Olivia. 2004. Organizational Culture War Games: Beyond Struggles for Intellectual Dominance. Word Document downloaded from:
http://www.sfu.ca/~tblawren/teaching/200509PHD987/Readings%20and%20res ources/Martin%20et%20al%20chapter.doc (23.11.07)

McCourt Perring, Christine. 1994. Community Care as De-Institutionalization? Continuity and Change in the Transition from Hospital to Community-Based Care. In: Wright, Susan (ed.). 1994. Anthropology of Organizations. London/ New York: Routledge. (168-180).

McKnight, John L. 1995. Why Servanthood is Bad. In: The Other Side, Vol. 31, No. 6. (38-40).

Menzel, Ulrich. 1992. Das Ende der dritten Welt und das Scheitern der großen Theorien. Frankfurt a.M. Suhrkamp.

Michels, Robert. 1966. Political Parties – A Sociological Study of the Oligarchical Tendencies of Modern Democracies. Toronto/ Ontario: Collier-MacMillan Canada.

Midgley, James. 1986. Introduction: Social Development, the State and Participation/ Community Participation: History, Concepts, and Controversies. In: Midgley, James (ed.). 1986. Community Participation, Social Development and the State. London/ New York: Methuen. (1-44).

Mkhatshwa, Smangaliso. 2007. The Role of Christian Churches in the Democratic South Africa. In: Kruip, Gerhard and Reifeld, Helmut (eds.). 2007. Church and Civil Society – The Role of Christian Churches in the Emerging Countries of Argentina, Mexico, Nigeria and South Africa. Sankt Augustin/ Berlin: Konrad Adenauer Stiftung. (127-134).

Mohan, Giles. 2007. Beyond Participation: Strategies for Deeper Empowerment. In: Cooke, Bill and Kothari, Uma (eds.). 2007 (4th impression). Participation: The new Tyranny? London/ New York: Zed Books. (153-167).

Mosse, David. 2001. Social Research in Rural Development Projects. In: Gellner, David N. and Hirsch, Eric (eds.). 2001. Inside Organizations – Anthropologists at Work. Oxford/ New York: Berg. (157-182).

Mosse, David and Lewis, David. 2006. Theoretical Approaches to Brokerage and Translation. In: Mosse, David and Lewis, David (eds.). 2006. Development Brokers and Translators: the Ethnography of Aid and Agencies. Bloomfield, CT: Kumarian Press (1-27).

Murdock, Donna F. 2003. That Stubborn „Doing Good?" Question: Ethical/ Epistemological Concerns in the Study of NGOs. In: Ethnos, Vol. 68, No. 4. (507-532).

Nader, Laura. 1974. Up the Anthropologist – Perspectives Gained from Studying Up. In: Hymes, Dell (ed.). 1974. Reinventing Anthropology. New York: Vintage Books. (284-311).

Nauta, Wiebe. 2006. Ethnographic Research in a NGO. In: Mosse, David and Lewis, David (eds.). 2006. Development Brokers and Translators: the Ethnography of Aid and Agencies. Bloomfield, CT: Kumarian Press (149-173).

Newling, Catherine. 2003. Mixe Responses to Neo-Liberalism: Questioning Sustainable Development as a Remedy to Free Trade and Global Capitalism in Oaxaca, Mexico. In: Dannhaeuser, Norbert and Werner, Cynthia (eds.). 2003. Anthropological Perspectives on Economic Development and Integration. Research in Economic Anthropology, Vol. 22. Oxford: ELSEVIER. (107-144).

Nolan, Riall W. 1994. Organizational Culture and the Development Crisis. In: Hamada, Tomoko and Sibley, Willis E. (eds.). 1994. Anthropological Perspectives on Organizational Culture. Lanham/ New York/ London: University Press of America. (373-396).

Novak, Andreas. 1994. Die Zentrale – ethnologische Aspekte einer Unternehmenskultur. Bonn: Holos Verlag.

Nuscheler, Franz. 2005. Entwicklungspolitik. Bonn: Lizenzausgabe für die Bundeszentrale für Politische Bildung.

Nustad, Knut G. 2001. Development: the Devil we Know? In: Third World Quarterly, Vol. 22, No. 4. (470-489).

O'Neill, Martin. 2001. Participation or Observation? Some Practical and Ethical Dilemmas. In: Gellner, David N. and Hirsch, Eric (eds.). 2001. Inside Organizations – Anthropologists at Work. Oxford/ New York: Berg. (221-230).

Osterman, Paul. 2006. Overcoming Oligarchy: Culture and Agency in Social Movement Organizations. In: Administrative Science Quarterly, Vol. 51, No. 4. (622-649).

Peters, Thomas, J. and Waterman, Robert, H. 1982. In Search of Excellence: Lessons from America's Best Run Companies. New York: Harper and Row Publishers.

Platteau, Jean-Phillippe and Gaspart, Frédéric. 2003. The Risk of Resource Misappropriation in Community Driven Development. In: World Development, Vol. 31, No. 10. (1687-1703).

Pretty, Jules N. 1995. Participatory Learning for Sustainable Agriculture. In: World Development, Vol. 23, No. 8. (1247-1263).

Prochnow, Martina. 1996. Entwicklungsethnologie: Ansätze und Probleme einer Verknüpfung von Ethnologie und Entwicklungshilfe. Zur Diskussion in der deutschsprachigen Ethnologie. Hamburg: LIT-Verlag.

Richards, Paul. 1995. Participatory Rural Appraisals: a Quick-and-Dirty Critique. In: PLA Notes, Issue 24. IIED London. (13-16).

Richards, Paul; Archibald, Steven; Beverlee, Bruce et al. 2005. Community Cohesion in Liberia. A Post-War Rapid Social Assessment. Social Development Papers (World Bank): Conflict Prevention and Reconstruction Unit, No. 21.

Richards, Paul; Bah, Khadija; Vincent, James. 2004. Social Capital and Survival: Prospects for Community-Driven Development in Post-Conflict Sierra Leone. Social Development Papers (World Bank): Community Driven Development Team, Conflict Prevention and Reconstruction Unit, No. 12.

Russel, Andrew and Edgar, Iain R. 1998. Research and Practice in the Anthropology of Welfare. In: Edgar, Iain R. and Russel, Andrew (eds.). 1998. The Anthropology of Welfare. London/ New York: Routledge. (1-15).

Russel, Andrew and Edgar, Iain R. (eds.). 1998. The Anthropology of Welfare. London/ New York: Routledge.

Sachs, Wolfgang (ed.). 1992. The Development Dictionary – A Guide to Knowledge as Power. London: Zed Books.

Schein, Edgar H. 2004. Organizational Culture and Leadership. 3rd edition. San Francisco: Jossey-Bass.

Schönhuth, Michael. 2002. Entwicklung, Partizipation und Ethnologie. Implikationen der Begegnung von ethnologischen und partizipativen Forschungsansätzen im Entwicklungskontext. (Universität) Trier: Fachbereich IV – Ethnologie. http://deposit.ddb.de/cgi-bin/dokserv?idn=974073318&dok_var=d1&dok_ext=pdf&filename=974073318.pdf (26.11.07)

Schönhuth, Michael. 1996. RRA und PRA. Gedanken zur Standortbestimmung und möglichen kulturwissenschaftlichen Perspektiven eines partizipativen Analyse-, Planungs- und Beratungsansatzes nach 15 Jahren in der Praxis. In: Bliss, Frank and Neumann, Stefan (eds.). 1996. Ethnologische Beiträge zur Entwicklungspolitik. Bonn: PAS. (13-37).

Schönhuth, Michael; Hess, Carmen; Sodeik, Eva; de Vries, Sandra. 1998. Mit den Augen des Ethnographen - Über den Einsatz partizipativer Methoden im Kontext von Forschung, Erhebung und Aktion. http://www.uni-trier.de/uni/fb4/ethno/publikationen/partizipation_lupe.pdf (25.03.07)

Schönteich, Martin and Louw, Antoinette. 2001. Crime in South Africa: A country and cities profile. Occasional Paper No 49 – 2001. Crime and Justice Programme, Institute for Security Studies. http://www.iss.org.za/pubs/papers/49/Paper49.html (14.01.07)

Sen, Amartya. 2000. Development as Freedom. New York: Alfred A. Knopf.

SLE (Seminar für Ländliche Entwicklung) / Fiege, Karin (editorial staff). 2003. Approaches to Reduce Youth Poverty in Cape Town, South Africa. Schriften-reihe des SLE, Humboldt Universität zu Berlin.

Sehring, Jennifer. 2002. Post-Washington Consensus und PRSP – Wende in der Weltbankpolitik? Hausarbeit zur Erlangung des Akademischen Grades einer Magistra Artium. Fachbereich Sozialwissenschaft: Johannes Gutenberg-Universität Mainz.

Senge, Peter M. 1990. The Fifth Discipline – The Art and Practice of the Learn-ing Organization. New York/ London: Currency Doubleday.

Shore, Cris. 2005. Culture and Corruption in the EU: Reflections on Fraud, Nepotism and Cronyism in the European Commission. In: Shore, Cris and Hal-ler, Dieter (eds.). 2005. Corruption – Anthropological Perspectives. London/ Ann Harbor: Pluto Press.

Smircich, Linda. 1983. Concepts of Culture and Organizational Analysis. In: Administrative Science Quarterly, Vol. 28, No.3. (339-358).
Spradley, James P. 1979. The Ethnographic Interview. New York/ Chicago etc.: Holt, Rhinehart and Winston.

Taylor, Harry. 2007. Insights into Participation from Critical Management and Labour Process Perspective. In: Cooke, Bill and Kothari, Uma (eds.). 2007 (4th impression). Participation: The new Tyranny? London/ New York: Zed Books. (122-138).

The Times English Dictionary. 2000. Glasgow: HarperCollins Publishers.

Thorbecke, Erik. 2006. The Evolution of the Development Doctrine, 1950-2005. Research Paper 2006/ No. 155. Helsinki: UNI-WIDER (United Nations Univer-sity, World Institute for Development Economics Research). http://www.wider.unu.edu/publications/rps/rps2006/rp2006-155.pdf (30.10.07)

Van Rooy, Alison. 1998. Civil Society and Democratisation: Wishful Thinking? In: Griffith, Ann L. (ed.). 1998. Building Peace and Democracy in Post-Conflict Societies. Center for Foreign Policy Studies. Dalhouse University. (15-30).

Van Ufford, Philip Q. 1993. Knowledge and Ignorance in the Practice of Devel-opment Policy. In: Hobart, Mark (ed.). 1993. An Anthropological Critique of Development – The Growth of Ignorance. London/ New York: Routledge. (135-160).

Verron, René; Williams, Glynn; Corbridge, Stuart et al. 2006. Decentralized Corruption or Corrupt Decentralisation ? Community Monitoring of Poverty-Alleviation Schemes in Eastern India. In: World Development, Vol. 34, No. 11. (1922-1941).

Waddington, Mark and Mohan, Giles. 2004. Failing Forward: Going beyond PRA and Imposed Forms of Participation. In: Hickey, Sam and Mohan, Giles (eds.). 2004. Participation – From Tyranny to Transformation? Exploring New Approaches to Participation in Development. London/ New York: Zed Books. (219-234).

West, Katarina. 2001. Agents of Altruism – The Expansion of Humanitarian NGOs in Rwanda and Afghanistan. Aldershot, Burlington etc.: Ashgate.

Wischmann, Meike. 1999. Angewandte Ethnologie und Unternehmen – Die praxisorientierte ethnologische Forschung zu Unternehmenskulturen. Münster, Hamburg, London: LIT Verlag.

Woost, Michael. 1997. Alternative Vocabularies of Development? Community and Participation in Development Discourse in Sri Lanka. In: Grillo, Ralph D. and Stirrat, Roderick L. (eds.). 1997. Discourses of Development. Anthropological Perspectives. Oxford/ New York: Berg (229-253).

World Bank. 1996. The World Bank Participation Sourcebook. Washington: IBRD/ World Bank.

Wright, Susan[1]. 1994. Culture in Anthropology and Organizational Studies. In: Wright, Susan (ed.). 1994. Anthropology of Organizations. London, New York: Routledge. (1-34).

Wright[2], Susan. 1994. Part III: Clients and Empowerment – Introduction. In: Wright, Susan (ed.). 1994. Anthropology of Organizations. London, New York: Routledge. (161-167).

Yin, Robert K. 1994. Case Study Research – Design and Methods. Second Edition. Applied Social Research Methods Series Volume 5. Thousand Oaks, CA et al.: Sage Publications.

96

Internet

Gesellschaft für Technische Zusammenarbeit:
www.gtz.de/de/publikationen/begriffswelt-
gtz/de/include.asp?lang=D&file=2_14.inc (29.10.07)

Official Website of Tshwane:
www.tshwane.gov.za/ (14.01.08)

Statistics South Africa - Quarterly Employment Statistics, December 2007:
www.statssa.gov.za/publications/P0277/P0277December2007.pdf (07.04.08)

The New Housing Policy and Strategy for South Africa:
www.info.gov.za/whitepapers/1994/housing.htm (18.02.08)

Tshwane Leadership Foundation:
www.tlf.org.za (20.02.08)

World Bank:
www.worldbank.org/empowerment (29.10.07)